Soccer Training for Girls

Acknowledgements:

For reasons of clarity and simplicity this book has been written sometimes using the male and sometimes the female form of address. However this refers to both sexes.

Klaus Bischops/Heinz-Willi Gerards

SOCCER TRAINING
FOR GIRLS

Meyer & Meyer Sport

Original title: Mädchenfußball
– Aachen: Meyer & Meyer, 2000
Translated by Anne Lammert

British Library Cataloguing in Publication Data
A catalogue for this book is available from the British Library

Bischops/Gerards
Soccer Training for Girls
– Oxford: Meyer und Meyer, (UK) Ltd., 2003
ISBN 1-84126-097-5

© 2003 by Meyer & Meyer Sport (UK) Ltd.
Aachen, Adelaide, Auckland, Budapest, Graz, Johannesburg,
Miami, Olten (CH), Oxford, Singapore, Toronto
Member of the World
Sports Publishers' Association
www.w-s-p-a.org

Printed and bound by Finidr – s. r. o., Český Těšín
ISBN 1-84126-097-5
E-Mail: verlag@m-m-sports.com
www.m-m-sports.com

List of Contents

FOREWORD

A Partner For Girls – The Ball

The idea of the game is the same for all and there are no fundamental differences in training theory for girls' and boys' Soccer as regards techniques and tactics. Differences can however be seen in the concept of play. For example one can observe the moral concepts of our society as far as specific female and male roles are concerned, which have led to role-specific development and therefore also to the evidence of typical girls' games.

Girls just don't play with a ball as often, in many cases they are even afraid of this round thing. This leads to initial weaknesses as regards ball control, passing is inaccurate and tackling and ball challenging behaviour is not developed enough.

However, on the other hand, girls fulfil the requirements that are essential for playing Soccer. They are more adroit, agile and flexible. They play with less physical emphasis but instead are very sensitive and adapt to situations. One seldom sees aggressive behaviour. They like to work cooperatively and learn more quickly, more intensively and with more endurance. Their motto is: work more with each other than against each other! Team spirit is their goal.

Sometimes with younger girls there is a strong 'bonding' to one person, and when the trainer is able to motivate the girls and handle them the right way, she can be sure to have enthusiastic active soccer players around her.

The training sessions explained in this book are designed to help make a well-motivated team become a successful team, who really enjoy playing Soccer.

Klaus Bischops
Heinz-Willi Gerards

1   SOCCER –
A FAVOURITE SPORT FOR GIRLS

In the USA, Girls' Soccer has long since been catapulted up to become the favourite girls' sport and in no time at all has managed to reach the top of the popularity scale for sports. In Europe, more and more girls are playing Soccer too but there isn't the same enthusiasm for girls' Soccer in the sports clubs on this side of the Atlantic as there is in the high schools in the USA.

Obviously the last Women's Soccer World Championship in the USA brought that expected bonus so that a sport which was more or less unpopular up to a few years ago was suddenly spread across the land with a storm of enthusiasm enabling it to bloom and flourish everywhere. Soccer for girls is IN, Soccer is CHIC, one ought to, or better, one just has to take part. But what is it, we'd like to know, that makes Soccer for girls so attractive and interesting and such an experience?

- The 'Team Game' Experience
  A Soccer team, where the same sports target is pursued by all, enables girls in school or club teams to be in a group of the same age, in which the out-of-school interests and life situations are similar. The exchanging of opinions, not to mention the social experience gained, both of which are important for many other situations in life, not only offers chances and opportunities in sport but in one's non-sporting life too. It is possible to build friendships in a team and experience personal aversions at the same time. Girls appreciate this know-how as it gives them enough scope to be able to go about their individual interests and needs.

> In short: As much team spirit as is required and is
> beneficial to personal development.

- The 'Combination Game' Experience
  The social aspect of Soccer as a team game can be seen in the combination game in particular. Girls' natural playful movements and their talent for sleek and coordinated shapes when running make combination with the ball easier and prevent actions, which demand or even gnaw at one's strength. The combination game enables them to exploit their chances.

- **Technique Experience**
  Many girls definitely find Soccer suitable as a game for them, because the use of technical elements meets with their own skills. Being able to deal skilfully with the apparatus 'ball', agility and manoeuvrability with the other girls on the pitch, confrontation with girls from the opposite team, as well as good body control with each new game situation; these are all criteria for a game based on technique.

  The girls' movements with the ball are rhythmic and flowing. They prefer low passes in a game and seldom employ high kicks and headers.

- **Running Experience**
  The physical requirements for young girls fit in well with the running mobility found in 'Soccer'. Different speed and forms of strain are constantly alternating, ranging from the slow motion trot to endurance running and on to more or less the long sprint. A player can control her intensity and endurance in running in accordance with her own fitness level. With growing playing experience, a player will then be able to distribute her potential performance more sensibly.

- **Combat Experience**
  Anyone who prefers using technical and playful methods in a game, will only go into 'combat' where it is either necessary or unavoidable. Thanks to this basic attitude – certainly not always conscious, more intuitive – the number of combat situations drops significantly.

  However, girls want to and have to fight for the ball, as Soccer is first and foremost a game of dual combat and exists from a succession of dual or 'multiple' combat situations. Success in this area can indeed decide a game and make a player more self-confident and give him more drive.

  Girls prefer a game with less physical emphasis, so that strength and toughness are not the essential requirements. Instead they draw on playful methods, such as quick passing and nimble dribbling. 'Out-playing' the opponent at the first signs of combat means fewer borderline situations and fewer interruptions to the flow of play by aggresive fouls during the game.

- **Game Rules Experience**
  Soccer, just like any other form of sport has certain rules. However it is possible to interpret the rules. They produce and provoke decisive situations for the players.

In this way the game offers each player scope for developing her own creativity and self-initiative. It's this very opportunity, which fits in with the attitude to life that young female athletes have.

- Time Experience
  Unlike basketball or volleyball there are no time-outs in Soccer where the trainer is able to brief or advise the players. This is only possible during half-time. The only chance for rectifying any errors is at this stage or before the next game at the latest.

The aspect of limited playing time can be particularly helpful for young people, girls especially, who in the course of a game are subject to physical as well as sometimes emotional processes. So – let's make things better!

Summary
The game of Soccer is beneficial to the entire physical and mental development process in young girls. It promotes those skills, which are necessary for one's life, improves skills in coordinating movement and shows ways of coping with mental decisive situations. Playing Soccer in a team is of course a lot of fun too.

FIFA referee Elke FIELENBACH, who refereed the German Soccer Federation Women's Cup Final in Berlin in 1999: "Women's Soccer is really different. Less emphasis on physical strength, not as dynamic, not as athletic but technically much better than the men's game – and much fairer. I show yellow/red cards three times more often during a men's match than during a women's one."

What Girls Bring Into a Game of Soccer

- Endurance in Competition

- Enthusiasm for the Game

- Action and Commitment in Battle

- Fitness

- Joy of Movement

- Offensive Playing Attitude

- Willingness to take Risks

- Speed

- Social Competence

- Joy of Playing

- Playing Ideas/Wit

- Technical Skills

- Goal Scoring

- Feminine Elegance

2 TRAINING WITH GIRLS – A REAL PLEASURE!

Soccer remains Soccer, whether played by children, girls, boys, men or women. It's defined by the rules of the game, age categories, competitions, training content among other things. Thus: a low pass stays a low pass and dribbling is always dribbling.

And yet we can say that the emphasis in Soccer varies according to the participants involved. Age, performance capacity, attitude to the game and many other factors all play a part. For this reason it is advisable, for those who plan and organise training and accompany the teams in a match, to have a good knowledge of Soccer.

Theory 1
It is quite possible that the state of performance in girls' teams is dissimilar. This depends on natural abilities, level of training and playing experience to date.

Theory 2
At certain stages of development girls are to a certain degree liable to experience an 'off-phase' in their attitude to the game of Soccer. Various factors can cause them to lose interest in a particular thing, which in turn leads them to become rapidly enthusiastic about a new idea and adamantly turn their back on what was their hobby up to now.

Theory 3
New friendships off the pitch or the feeling of a loss in prestige within the team can sometimes cause girls to stop playing Soccer, even when the commitment to the team appears to be fixed.

Theory 4
Girls have their own rhythm of life, which is more or less strongly influenced by the people around them. A change in their sphere of influence can can cause a fluctuation in interests too.

For example, if one is planning to work with a group of girls and wants this group to become a real team in training and in matches, then the trainer must be able to recognise and 'treat' any factors of development, which can endanger this

team. The more thorough and intensive the sense of belonging to the team is, the less likely it is that a process of detachment will set in.

Thus each individual trainer has a whole host of chances – be it pedagogic or directly Soccer related – of uniting the girls as tightly as possible with the game of 'Soccer' and their team.

The following 'building blocks' offer trainers and assistants practical help for best dealing with situations of conflict.

Building Block 1
The girls should **feel comfortable** in their training and match group. Good vibes within the team encourage remarkable and adventurous activities off the pitch.

Building Block 2
In the sporting sector one should combine the **fun of playing Soccer** with the trainer's demands as far as possible so that the trainer's personal intentions come to fruition. In certain age groups for example, an improvement can be achieved mainly through play or through the introduction of certain playful elements.

Building Block 3

The structure of every training session should be **varied and variable** and include unexpected and surprise elements. The girls should feel encouraged to add in their own ideas. This increases their willingness to take risks and makes them more courageous and less predictable in a match.

This creative and playful scope, which should be affordd to each player, is what guarantees long-term interest in Soccer.

Building Block 4

The girls should at least be able to play in **different positions** in training. They improve their playing qualities and gain experience, two requirements which benefit the team game. As well as this, training then offers variety and depth and ensures that each player learns to play both offensively and defensively.

Building Block 5

Numerous analyses show that Soccer players reach mostly only average fitness levels, unlike other competitive athletes. This is bound to stem perhaps from the type of training that they carry out − with the emphasis on Soccer itself and therefore without much variety.

Girls who are interested in several other forms of exercise are good potential candidates for a more **varied interpretation of movement** in the area of fitness training, e.g. gymnastics to music or with a ball, modern dance forms and other methods of fitness training.

In this way they achieve good overall agility, take sensible measures towards the prevention of injuries and are able to cope with extreme situations of play with less effort involved.

Building Block 6

There is no doubt that the emphasis of basic training is on the development of **technical skills** and a good **sense of play** within a team. In order to be able to rationally get the girls not to be shy of the ball, be skilful when tackling and challenging, or to pass the ball freely and sometimes often with a risk − this often comes off effectively − all serving to strengthen the girls' initiative. To do this certain provocative tasks are necessary. Small competitions with innovative exercises or goal-scoring games in a marked off area of the pitch, with built-in special tasks, increase the girls' motivation and enjoyment of the game.

3 DEVELOPMENT PSYCHOLOGY – THIS IS WHAT YOU OUGHT TO KNOW

Play and training for young people should follow the conditions and requirements for learning and performance, which have proven to be particularly effective in the prevailing development phase. Knowledge of the characteristic features of the development phase in question is also a relevant factor when training girls according to their age. For this reason, from day one, girls' training is not merely women's training, which has been reduced in duration or load levels.

Development phases in children and adolescents seldom follow a straight line. It lifts up and down, back and forward and contains occasional traceable signs of progress, but also standstills and apparent set-backs. The development phases do not take place at the same time for each individual, thus relatively large differences are visibly evident among children of the same age. There are discrepancies between calendar and biological age. So for example an eight-year old, who has the same physical stature as a ten-year old girl, is not at the corresponding psychological stage of development.

Knowledge of development psychology characteristics enables the trainer to allocate her training stimuli hand in hand with development levels. One knows however, that there are development phases of childhood and adolescence, in which girls react more intensively, appear more open for learning material and are thus are able to achieve a higher level of success in learning or performance.

In his book "Endurance Training" (German edition, 1988, p. 179) Fritz ZINTL looks at this subject:

> "Every stage of development has its biological features and advantages regarding the extent of training on conditional and motor abilities. We know from the characteristics of certain age groups that;
> - early school age (6/7-10 years) is favourable for the acquirement of motor skills and for the improvement of coordination skills
> - later school age (11-12 years) is the best learning age for target-oriented practice of basic sport techniques
> - due to the growing phase, puberty (12-14 years) and adolescence (14-17 years) are very suited to the improvement of fitness."

One cannot split up the various development phases exactly, as all transitional phases flow into each other.

Four-step Model of Development Phases

Age	Development Phase	Intention of Training	Training Emphasis
5-9/10 years	Primary school age	Girls enjoy playing Soccer	Varied basic sports training: getting used to the ball, ball games, running, jumping, throwing, gymnastics, exercises, dancing, simple basic techniques in Soccer.
9/10-11/12 years	Pre-puberty phase, best learning age	Our game has to get better	Technique training, acquiring rough, principles/skills, corrections, improvement, and refinement of skills
11/12-13/14 years	Puberty phase, growth in height	What has been learnt is stabilised	Diversified training, firming of the various techniques, working on fitness abilities, stabilisation of coordination ability.
14-17 years	Second puberty phase	Girls play competitive Soccer	Improvement of technique, gearing training towards competition, working out an individual style of play.

Some Words of Comment

- Starting off playing Soccer
  Girls and boys gain skill in the period between 7 and 11 years old, during which there is a strong development in coordination skills. It is almost impossible to catch up later on any learning advantage that can be reached at this age. Girls who start playing Soccer at a later age have a Soccer-specific agility deficiency in many cases. If the girls start playing Soccer at a younger age, they have exactly the same chances of learning as boys. Not only that, they are often a hair's breadth ahead of the boys as far as coordination skills are concerned, because the muscles and the nervous system work together excellently for all movements.

- Co-educational Soccer
  It is of course possible for girls and boys to train and play Soccer together up until they are 10 years old, as the development process relating to movement-specific playing characteristics such as flexibility, speed and endurance run similarly for both.

- The fun of Soccer
  The primary target when training with girls is to arouse their interest in the game of Soccer, to keep up this interest and intensify it. Constant variety in training, regular new ideas for playing and varied forms of movement as well as tasks for groups and teams all serve this purpose.

- The trainer's competence
  Children and girls principally learn things through imitation. This means that the trainer must be capable of demonstrating technical and play processes correctly in order to be able to convey the trainer's intentions. Not only this, linguistic qualities are important when explaining such processes; these two factors combined are what give the trainer specialist competence.

  Apart from specific knowledge in word and action she always has an educational role in bringing up these children. Some girls will see the trainer as a model figure, a fact that the trainer should be aware of.

  In training it might be perfectly suitable in some situations for the trainer to take a back seat somewhat and give the girls scope for bringing in their own forms of movement and play. Girls' involvement in training, no matter what form it takes, can liven up and stimulate the programme.

Encouragement as well as praise in training and during a match are good ways of keeping the girls loyal to the game of Soccer and their team. Young girls react sensitively to negative comments or the pointing out of specific individual mistakes. Their enjoyment of the game is dampened somewhat. Individual criticism of adolescent girls can lead to overreactions, which can damage the team. Specific words of criticism and the correction of individual errors are best done in groups of twos or threes in as positive an atmosphere as possible.

The atmosphere in training and during a match should be open, relaxed and honest, but without forgetting the necessary amount of concentration. As a result the girls will be bound to involve themselves and be enthusiastic about training and matches.

- **The targets in matches and in training**
  As well as the prime target of having a "fun game", the girls gain a lot of experience for life as regards getting on with people of the same age e.g. team spirit, independence, feeling of responsibility, learning how to deal with diferent people, fairness, acceptance of decisions, being able to win and lose.

3.1   Girls at Primary School Age

The essential elements for training girls up to the age of 10 years old is fun and enjoyment of the game. The young players belong to a team because they want to play Soccer. They know nothing about tactical behaviour as yet and the other girls around them don't play an important role at this stage. Playing Soccer means: the ball has be got into the other team's goal and of course every girl wants to do this herself where possible. For this reason one must plan and carry out training in such a way that the girls are interested and enthusiastic about the whole thing and that they all love coming to training.

At the beginning, all players run around with or after the ball. Each girl knows only that the ball has to land in the other team's goal. Playing together with someone or passing to someone is more of a coincidence than anything else, and is seldom planned. However girls at this age quickly and easily learn new skills, thus constantly improving their game.

The desire for movement that many girls have enables varied basic training in the game form. Practice and training at this age is always disguised with playful elements.

Ten passes for a good girls' training session
- The main focus of training is on **techno-motor education**. Basic movements such as running, jumping, throwing, climbing, shooting, dribbling and passing are the core of this 'playful work'.

- The basic forms of all technical elements to be learned are always taught in **the form of a game**, relays, small competitions. The trainer selects simple procedures which are easy for the children to understand. Easing the rules also raises the enjoyment when practising.

- Training takes place in **small groups** where the trainer can have a watchful eye on all players and where a lot of ball contact is possible. It is this aspect that is particularly important when learning technical skills. Where possible every child should have a ball to herself for technique training.

- **Using a different ball** – instead of a Soccer, a tennis ball or rugby ball is used – naturally offers new playing experience, which makes the girls even more enthusiastic. Training exercises, which are varied in content are an optimal source of motivation in training.

- The word **"fitness"** does not play any role at all for players at this age, as they're hardly unstoppable as long as the play-oriented training is fun for them. Although children have a good aerobic load tolerance, endurance training is hardly effective at all. Instead of this, fitness, agility, speed of reaction and speed in games, relays and other forms of movement are all worked on in a totally natural way.

- **"Demonstrating"** in training often has a longer lasting effect and has a better chance of bringing success than a mere explanation. The girls don't want to hear long theoretical explanations; they want to play and try things out. After the trainer has demonstrated something the girls start trying this out immediately. In order to correct any errors at a later stage the technical procedure is repeated again with the players and finally practised together with them. When correction is necessary the advice given should always have a notably positive touch and be directed at all players. Criticism or even scolding is something that the girls are hardly able to understand as they feel they have done their best.

- **Learning social behaviour** should also be an essential aspect of training. While in their first playing attempts, the girls may see only the ball and perceive team colleagues or the players of the opposite team to be mere obstacles in their bid to score a goal. As they gather more playing experience they will realise that one's team colleagues can be very useful and supportive in the achievement of the 'goal scoring' target. As well as this, the atmosphere before and after training or a match has a decisive influence on a team's togetherness.

- **One constantly changes playing positions** both in training and in a match. This means that there is variety in training. It enables the players to get a good look at the process of a game in its entirety as well as the demands and difficulties of particular playing positions. Only someone who has stood in the goal can understand why the goalkeeper sometimes misses the ball. In the course of time one can see what each girl's favourite playing position is.

  Trainers who allocate specific playing positions from very early on are depriving the girls of variety in training and are thus narrowing their scope for experience.

- The aim of the game form in training sessions is the use of **both feet** from the very beginning. For this reason every exercise in training should be carried out with both the right and the left foot. Being able to kick with both feet is of significant advantage in many match situations.

* The term **"tactics"** has no significance for girls of this age. What's more important here is the courage to try things out, showing one's wit in play and the developments arising from this love of play. Every form of tactical advice normally meets with misunderstanding, it inhibits the enjoyment of playing and is meaningless when one considers that the opposing players are not working with tactics either; girls just want to play Soccer.

3.2   Girls during the Pre-pubescent Phase

The phase between primary school age and the beginning of puberty (9/10 – 11/12 years) is referred to as the pre-pubescent stage of development. Girls grow at a relatively steady pace both in height and girth and all organs adapt to this development. So in this growing phase they show harmonious and adaptable movement. This is the best time for a successful learning situation. The girls don't dally long about things, they simply try out the techniques and movement sequences demonstrated and can normally master them within a very short time.

The central focus of training here is on the improvement of Soccer techniques, provided that this is built into a game situation. The girls themselves have a lot of scope for development when this takes place in small groups, where they can have frequent ball contact in a variety of exercises and games.

Two factors are required for technique training:
* Concentrated frequent repetition in various different game situations, so that the movement sequences become automatic; what we're talking about here is the coordination of the muscular and central nervous systems.
* Technique training requires game concept orientation and the reinforcement of this in a real game situation; one learns to play Soccer by playing with the football!

A trainer should explain and demonstrate the entire range of technical possibilities and practise them in a realistic way.

- The girls get to know the game's basic situations, such as taking shots, defence, ball control, dribbling and cooperation, learn about technical possibilities and how to deal with them, thus acquiring their first real tactical view of the game.

- The question of how to tackle the technical demands can be properly answered by the principle of learning to play with both feet. Fundamental techniques for playing with one's head or other 'permitted' parts of the body are also acquired. Any corrections that are necessary are short, precise and relevant in manner.

- Coordinative elements, as well as nimbleness and agility, determine the quality of play to a particular extent. These skills can now be quite successfully taught in combination with technical processes.

- According to DE MAREES, girls react and adapt to endurance loads from 10 years old onwards. In spite of this, separate fitness training is not necessary as the central game concept is effective here.

- Trainers working with this age group have to be good technicians in order to be able to demonstrate all technical procedures correctly. Training at this point in particular should be innovative and variable and can even include competition concepts. Where possible one should work in small groups and any assistance or correction necessary is conveyed with understanding. Encouragement, recognition and praise are the best motivators.

3.3   Girls during the First Phase of Puberty

A change of shape and build is the characteristic feature of the first phase of puberty. The start of growth in height indicates the end of the girls' successful learning age up until now. Trunk length and leg length develop out of proportion, so that movements seem to be disharmonious. This 'disproportion' makes it more difficult to learn new movement sequences. For this reason it is only possible to work on and strengthen elements, which have already been learnt where technique is concerned.

Working out new technical procedures becomes difficult and does not really lend much hope of any progress, particularly in motor behaviour. The noticeable differences in height demand differences in training.

- As regards technique, the main emphasis for girls during the first phase of puberty (11/12-13/14 years old) lies in reinforcing and stabilising those techniques already learnt. Exercises for coordination continue to play an important part just as before. At this point one can take a more intensive look at aspects relating to physical condition.

- At the same time there is a development in intellectual skills, although memory has reached its optimal intake ability from the age of 12. At this point the trainer can start with initial tactical training. In game situations the players try out some tactical manoeuvres on their own and tune in their own playing behaviour with teammates and players of the opposite team. This in turn can be practised in minority and majority situations, using varied forms and standard situations.

- The aspect of physical condition now grows in importance. Aerobic endurance loads and speed can be worked on effectively. Strength training should neither take the form of maximal performance nor strength endurance but rather through pull and push competitions, in skipping and pushing exercises. It takes place using body weight, light apparatus, a medicine ball or a skipping rope. Circuit training is also suitable at this age.

- Nimbleness and agility continue to be practised unrestrictedly. Speed training can be quite effective and can take the form of sprints, relays and reaction games.

- The trainer must be very sensitive when handling players in this age group. She must respect the girls' striving for independence and be willing to accompany them on their way to becoming an independent person. On the one hand, she is an expert on sport, but at the same time she should be an understanding companion, who is willing occasionally to withdraw and take a back seat. The girls react very sensitively to criticism; even if it can be objectively justified, it is often perceived as being hurtful and upsetting. The players prefer to be approached personally.

Even off the pitch the trainer is often invited to parties and meetings. She should therefore have a good sense of humour, be cheerful and easy-going around the players and allow them scope for putting things to the test themselves. In difficult situations, mostly only patience and tolerance help.

Enjoyment of the game and the sense of belonging to the team still have priority. Every player must have the feeling within her that her she is an indispensible part of the team. This is the case for "early developers", when, due to their growth in height, their motor behaviour appears immature and leads to errors. This also holds for 'late developers', who, because of physical development disadvantages, lack the necessary drive.

3.4   Girls during the Second Phase of Puberty

When this phase of development sets in, the girls' coordination skills improve, harmony returns and the movements become more feminine. Body girth firms up and the whole motory system seems to be in balance again. Thanks to harmonic body proportions and higher intellectual levels the players go through a second 'golden age of learning', making it possible for them to acquire new techniques and movement sequences under competitive conditions.

The emphasis in training is on the refinement of Soccer technique skills and on an improvement in physical fitness. One can notice a new willingness to learn and perform among the players. Having said this, however, there are sometimes fluctuations in performance, caused by the menstrual cycle or hormonal influences. Women trainers are certain to show understanding about this.

- Now, the techniques of the game and training under competitive conditions are practised. The pressures of time and opposing players should be clearly felt in the process. Techniques specifically for a particular playing position are now practised, although speed acceleration and precision play a role here. A personal playing style begins to develop.

- As regards tactics, the programme includes, apart from practice itself, the introduction and development of certain combinations of play on a flip-chart or on video. The players work out possible alternatives to this. The girls' personal involvement here means it's easier to put theory into practice. Other themes such as changes in tempo, in game emphasis, tackling and challenging among others are on the training programme.

- When working on physical condition, it is possible to start off with this from the age of 15 onwards. Maximal strength training is also reasonable although one should continue to avoid static support exercises.

Speed, resilience and endurance are pushed according to the type of sport in question. If one intends guiding the players towards top-level performance, then it is necessary to work on speed endurance in particular.

- The trainer can now take a step back and allow individual players, within the realms of their possibilities, build up their personality. Conversations serve to convey those tactics necessary in a match, and on the other hand, to solve any individual or team problem situations, which may arise.

- A basic fundamental factor is ensuring a positive attitude in the team, so that the players remain true to Soccer. At the end of adolescence, when the entire development is complete and in harmony, the trainer can then offer assistance for the changeover to women's Soccer.

4 TIPS FOR THE TRAINER

If the girls are to appreciate and relate well to the person responsible for training, then it is necessary for her to be particularly sensitive with players of a young age and be willing to deal with individual players more personally. The inclusion of the following points will help.

- Young female players strive for individual space and independence. They may be granted this freedom as long as there is no damage to the team spirit.

- The trainer must be the expert on the one hand, and on the other hand an understanding 'guardian', who is a sympathetic listener when the young women have problems.

- Girl players react very sensitively to criticism during puberty. They sometimes leave the team or turn their back on the whole sport altogether. Instead of this they hope for care and recognition. The trainer should talk privately with the player concerned as well as within a small group.

- The trainer should lead the young people to be responsible for themselves and offer them space and scope, both in training and in a match, to try things out for themselves.

- Praise, recognition and encouragement will always be the best forms of motivation there are for keeping a girl committed to Soccer in the long term.

- The trainer needs patience when dealing with her players; for this reason she should try and clear up precarious situations in a humorous manner.

- An overexaggerated sense of authority will hardly help in building a trusting relationship with her players. Specialist knowledge, competence and sensitivity are what convey the authority needed to achieve the right working atmosphere.

- If players are afforded the opportunity often in training to go about a task in a way that they would like to, it then enables them to bear in mind the development of different situations. At the same time, those particularly talented and high-performance players are given scope for developing their skills further by using their own iniative. Weaker players, on the other hand, have the chance to practise basic elements.

The following pedagogic principles should form the basis for starting girls off with Soccer:

1. The trainer tries to create a positive training and playing atmosphere.
2. She develops and promotes the girls' fun and involvement in training and games.
3. She breaks down the girls' fear of the ball and of the opposing player and motivates them with their own successful experiences.
4. She gives the players the opportunity to occupy themselves with the ball and to promote their creativity in play.
5. While conveying 'girlish' forms of movement she lays out training to be as varied as possible.

- Girls are mostly inexperienced when it comes to Soccer. Therefore, in the following, some basic principles of instruction are laid out, which make work with beginners easier.

The trainer
- gives the girls some basic experience of Soccer through similar games.
- uses balls which are suitable for girls, i.e. light ones.
- includes typical girls' apparatus in training such as hoops, short ropes, bands as well as music.
- draws on gymnastic exercises and stretching exercises in particular.
- works in groups, which are as small and manageable as possible, in order to raise training intensity.
- ensures and stabilises the girls' handling of the ball before including exercises for dealing with opponents.

- Finally, the trainer has to convey training content, which can be divided up into five areas:

P 1 Getting used to the Ball

The girls learn
- how a ball rolls, flies and hops.
- how a ball can move in the air and on the ground.
- how a ball is thrown and bounced.
- how a ball can be played with the foot, the head and other parts of the body.
- how a ball can be brought to a standstill.

P 2 Ball Control/Combination

The girls practise
- how to move the ball with the foot (left, right).
- how to play the ball flat, half-high and high to another player.
- how to take the ball when standing and on the move.
- how to pass the ball on directly.

P 3 Striking Technique/Shooting at Goal

The players practise
- the various striking techniques with a still and rolling ball.
- shots at goal, with and without a goalkeeper.
- shots over short and long distances.
- centre passes from the right and the left.
- shots at goal, with and without an opponent.

P 4 Defence/Build-up/Attack

The girls
- win back the ball from an opposing player.
- interrupt the opposing team in their combination and get ball possession.
- try to keep the ball amongst the own team.
- want to outplay an opponent.
- launch an attempt to pass into the open for a team member.
- play double passes with each other.
- kick a centre pass in front of the opponent's goal.

P 5 Standard Situations

A player
- lands the ball in front of the goal from a corner.
- does throw-ins.
- takes free kicks from different positions from the side and in front of the opponent's goal.
- takes penalty kicks.

5 COACHING IN TRAINING AND DURING A MATCH

Adequate care of the entire team as well as of the individual players – in short good, individual and team-related coaching – this is the most important requirement for binding girls to Soccer intensively and over a long term. The main priority in coaching is for matches and training, but quality coaching is always to do with the people themselves, and for this reason, it is not just limited to the time spent together in sport.

5.1 Coaching during Training

During routine training, the trainer strikes up contact with the team or individual players. This can occur at a time before, during or after training. However, being able to pick the right moment for this is a question of the trainer's tact.

For various reasons it can be necessary to have a talk with the whole team or team section. Similarly there may be grounds for talks individually one-to-one or with the whole training group present.

Likely reasons for talks and discussion
- The trainer recaps on the last match, characterising the team's play in the offensive and defensive areas. She includes the players in her discussion and asks them to describe either the performance within their own group (defence, centrefield, attack etc.) or general behaviour in certain game situations. Improvements in performance and successful combinations can be positively emphasised. The idea behind this discourse is not so much evaluation or even criticism, but rather a factual, objective account of particular situations.

- A certain apathy can be noticed during training (routine training). The trainer asks a few leading players in the team to think out and develop several new exercise ideas for the next training session (e.g. for the warm-up).

- When certain players start to stand out for behaviour which is damaging to the team (unpunctuality, unreliability, lack of concentration etc.), the trainer looks for definite ways, perhaps even together with other players, to get the girls back to be more interested and committed to the team.

- If a player is bothered by problems not related to sport (school, family situation, girlfriend, boyfriend), one can offer the opportunity to talk about this either within the team or with the trainer.

- Although training should be the time where the girls can relate their daily experiences to each other, the trainer can be a silent listener and willing conversation partner when problems arise.

5.2 Coaching during a Match

Every team has more players available than needed for a match. So even before the match begins, the trainer has to make certain decisions. Coaching can be divided up into the times before, during and after the match.

A Before the match

- The trainer must send the eleven strongest players – based on their training performance – for this particular game onto the pitch. All those players who have been picked must be able to run out with the feeling that the trainer has her full confidence in them.

- The subsitutes must also have the feeling that they are fully accepted members of the team, who can stand in for a player at any time. Even those girls who have not been picked must be able to cheer, celebrate and suffer with the team, in short, feel they belong to the team.

- The players meet punctually at the appointed rendezvous prior to the game. If a girl can't play, the trainer must be informed in good time.

- If it's an away match, one must check that the team is complete before heading off.

- Immediately after arriving at the venue one takes a look at the pitch in order to select the appropriate clothes and shoes (weather conditions, ground surface).

- After they have changed, the trainer sends the players out to warm up. The warm-up is either done individually or in small groups.

- Before kick-off the players gather together and psyche themselves up by shouting out together their rally cry.

B During the match

- The trainer watches the run of play. If a player's tasks are just asking too much of her, it may be necessary to change around within the team. If this measure doesn't help it is possible to bring on a substitute.

- A little tip can sometimes help a player to improve her game and get to grips better with her position.

- Praise from the trainer and positive words of encouragement are significantly more effective to spur on the girls' performance capability than criticism or even abuse.

C At half-time

- The players are calmed down first and any scrapes or wounds are seen to. They are given a drink to relax.

- After this short break it is now time to talk about the second half. Starting off with a short word on the team's performance up till now, the positive elements, in particular, are emphasised. Concrete errors are described briefly and corrected with some tips from the trainer. A possible new tactical route may be drawn up for the second half. Finally any planned substitutions are named and the reasons for this briefly mentioned. The girls are sent out into the second half with encouraging words.

D After the match

- When the team has won the match or managed an unexpected draw, the trainer shows delight with her players.

- If the game ends up in a defeat, whether deserved or just unfortunate, one does not give certain players the blame for this. Instead, the trainer gives her team some words of encouragement so that they are cheered up by the next training session.

- The trainer also joins in with the cooling down run together with the whole team, using the time for talks with the players.

6 STRUCTURE OF A TRAINING SESSION

The planning or structure of each practical session and how it's carried out is decided according to the trainer's personal concept. Having said this, what has proven to be effective and worthwhile in practice is a structural breakdown into three parts (Getting in the mood/Warm-up – Main emphasis training – Putting this into practice in a game). Firstly, it is easy to follow, enables good understanding of information and secondly allows enough room and scope to incorporate the players own skills and to consider any organisational points.

As regards content, one must heed the following basic principles:

Getting in the mood/Warm-up (15-25 min)

Aims
- Body and mind are prepared for the exertion that follows in the main training phase.
- The cardiovascular system is stimulated and brought to 'working temperature'.
- There is an emotional 'tuning in' to the demands that follow.
- Warming up serves to prevent injuries occurring.
- The muscular system is made supple through stretching exercises.

Contents
- Loose trotting.
- Gymnastic exercises with and without a ball.
- Exercises to help flexibility and nimbleness.
- Coordination exercises.
- Sprints, acceleration sprints (pick ups)
- Individual activity with the ball to improve the girls' feeling for the ball.
- Catching and running games.

A few hints
Even in the introductory phase of training, the warm-up, it is important to match the girls' specific interests:

- Gymnastic exercises with or without hand apparatus such as a ball, baton, rope, hoop are normally very popular.
- Stretching exercises and aerobics are very popular forms of movement with girls.
- Movement and gymnastics to music are another method of emotional tuning.

Main Emphasis Training (30-40 min)

Aims
- Technical skills are acquired, reinforced and refined.
- Playing elements are learnt and practised.
- Coordination and fitness elements are practised and strengthened again and again.
- Tactical aspects for the game are incorporated into play situations and then put into practice.

Contents
- Basic techniques like passing, blocking, heading.
- Individual, partner and group work with the ball.
- Exercises and games for reaction and speed.
- Various types of shots.
- Playing ball combinations together.
- Scoring and preventing goals.
- Minority and majority situation games.
- Defensive and offensive play.
- Tasks in the centrefield.

A few hints
The main emphasis training phase is for the girls to learn and improve their Soccer game. As well as just pure practice, it is important to have as many playing aspects as possible included. Motivating exercises/games are carried out according to methodic principles (from easy to difficult, from simple to complex), all leading to the target of playing Soccer.

It is recommended to pay attention to the following principles in the main emphasis training phase:

- Technique training always takes place before fitness training, as it is almost impossible for the players to concentrate properly when they are tired.

- Speed training on the other hand takes place best, right at the beginning of main emphasis training, directly after an intensive warm-up.
- Endurance training is best done at the end of the session, and this can be carried out also as game play.

Training – Put into Practice in a Game (15 - 25 min)

Aims
- The elements learnt in the emphasis training phase are now used in a game.
- Contents dealt with in previous emphasis training phases are now tried out, built on and reinforced in a game.
- The training elements learnt are put to use under competitive conditions.

> Contents
> - Games one on one up to 5-aside.
> - Games with majority and minority situations.
> - Cooperation within individual team sections.
> - Defence against attack.
> - Playing with the whole team.
> - Game under competitive conditions.
> - Game with special tasks (e.g. marking a player, marking a space, running for passes etc).

A few hints
The playing phase at the end of a training session is characterised mainly by a sense of achievement and leaves behind a general positive atmosphere. The good mood achieved strengthens the players' interest in the game of Soccer as well as giving them fresh motivation for the next activity.

Cool-down Run (10-15 min)

Although the training breakdown into the three phases does not include a cooling down run after training and competition as a specific element in its structure, it is an indispensable requirement. Cooling down must follow a match or a heavy training session and it takes the form of relaxed trotting, running and a number of relaxing and loosening exercises. Movement involving dancing or gymnastics are also suitable for girls.

In the practical training sessions later on in this book there is no particular reference made to the cooling down run.

7 A FEW WORDS ON THE SUBJECT OF COORDINATION

The significance and value of coordination training has become an ever-increasing object of attention for Soccer experts recently. It's understandable really, as playing Soccer means running, jumping, playing and competing with a round piece of apparatus, namely – a ball – which can be used in plenty of different ways – and against other players who are fighting for ball possession. For this activity, coordination skills are definitely what is called for and very handy in the course of a game.

Coordination in Soccer refers to the ability to keep control of the ball when under attack from an opposing player. In order to fulfil this essential requirement as best as possible for a successful game, it's imperative that coordination training plays a role in each training session.

- Coordination can only be improved when one is fresh. For this reason it is a regular part of the warm-up phase. It can also be dealt with as an essential building block at the beginning of the main emphasis training phase.

- Many exercises aimed at improving ball technique also improve coordination at the same time.

- Just how fast and complex the coordination exercises are varies from player to player and must be adapted appropriately. Exercises that are too easy are hardly going to lead to any performance improvement; exercises that are too advanced take the fun out of working with a ball.

- Particularly suitable for improving coordination are combination and complex exercises, which require flexibility on the part of the players due to the fundamental changes in task.

- Incorrect movements should be corrected immediately so that they don't creep in over the long term.

- Coordination training will be varied and challenging when many different forms of apparatus are used. Having said this, the ball plays the leading role in each training session; then again it is possible to use balls of all shapes and sizes for this training.

8 SOME POINTS OF ADVICE FOR PUTTING THINGS INTO PRACTICE

Such a breakdown may seem unconventional, but nevertheless playing Soccer can be divided up into five areas, which are a concrete part of the training programme.

- BF   Ball Familiarisation
- DB   Dribbling – Ball control
- ST   Shooting techniques – Types of shots
- OD   Offensive and defensive behaviour
- SS   Standard situation

Despite dividing up a complex game into individual elements for emphasis in training, it is clear that all the other elements of the game in each area must be practised as well. The complex character of the game remains intact even with particularly intensive training on one individual point. For the sake of the game itself, practising individual elements must be subordinate to the principle of 'complexity'. This can be achieved when individual exercise elements are combined together in a game context as soon as possible.

This basic concept offers a general guideline for incorporating structure into the game played, with of course the knowledge that street footballers are capable of learning how to play brilliant Soccer through 'learning by doing' without such structures and without a trainer's guidance. There is no specific methodical background to the structure illustrated in this book. One can select randomly from the various training sessions. However, the fact must not be ignored that sometimes particular skills are required for the optimal achievement of certain objectives.

The five areas of training are not categorised according to age or playing skills. It can be assumed that the trainer can adapt every training session – within certain allowances or alterations and added difficulties – to fit in with any training group's level.

A lot of importance is attached to coordination training. The intensive training of coordination elements makes it easier, firstly, to pick up new technical skills and, secondly, fits in particularly well with girls' interests. For this reason coordination elements can be included both in the introduction to the training session as well as in the main emphasis training phase.

8.1 Ball Familiarisation – Ten Training Sessions

Lack of activity as well as lack of experience with the 'piece of leather' soon make it clear that playing and working with the ball, i.e. getting used to the ball, is a relevant criterium for learning how to play Soccer. For this reason 'familiarisation' is sometimes understandably referred to as the primary school for playing Soccer. With the help of ten training sessions the trainer can show her players how to get familiar with the ball and its features.

BF 1

Getting into the Mood/Warming up

Exercise with the skipping rope
Each player takes a skipping rope.
The skipping rope is a piece of equipment, which is particularly liked by girls. They will be able to develop many different creative movement possibilities by themselves.

Exercises on the spot
- Swing the rope backward or forward and skip.
- Skip with and without steps in between.
- Two players skip in one rope.
- While skipping do a slow full turn.
- Skip on one foot.

Exercises on the move
- The girls run and swing the ropes in one and twostep rhythm.
- Swinging the rope as you hop along.
- With a side gallop, the girls jump into the swinging rope .

Combinations
- Now the girls think out their own combinations by joining different exercises together. Stretching exercises with the skipping rope take place between the individual exercises.

Emphasis Training

Playing and exercising with the gymnastics ball
Girls are mostly familiar with the gymnastics ball. They have often used it before and thus know its features.
- The ball is bounced, first with the right and then with the left hand. This is done on the spot first and then on the move.
- While bouncing the ball the girls run around, do full turns, do hook shots, constantly change their direction, getting slower and then faster.
- Shadowing each other, the girls run around bouncing the ball, imitating the movements of the person in front of them.
- While running around with the ball the players bounce the ball from the right hand to the left.
- The ball is thrown up in the air while running and then caught again.
- The ball is thrown up in the air and then caught in a jump.
- The ball is lightly kicked forward and should stay as close to the foot as possible.
- Keeping the ball by the foot, it is then dribbled in a circle, in a figure eight or round a square.
- The ball is kept up in the air for as long as possible.
  Who can manage three contacts with the ball in a row without the ball touching the ground?

Putting it into Practice in a Game

Relay forms
Depending on the number of players, two or three relay teams are formed, and start beside each other.
- From the starting line the ball is dribbled as fast as possible around a turning point and back again.
- Along the distance to be dribbled, more cones are put down and the girls have to dribble around these, as in a slalom.

Cool-down run

BF 2

Getting in the Mood/Warm-up

Playing with the gymnastics ball
One practises with a partner, so that two girls always have a gymnastics ball between them.
- The players throw the ball to each other, first with the right hand and then with the left, and catch it.
- After throwing the ball to the other girl, the thrower does a spin turn.
- While running around, the girls throw the ball to each other. One must be careful to avoid bumping into other couples.
- While running around, the ball is bounced to each other.
- The girls pass the ball to each other on the spot.
- The passing activity is continued, but the distance between the girls increases.
- After passing the ball, the girl jumps into a crouch position and then stands up again immediately.
- While trotting around, the ball is passed down low to each other.
- Both partners try to get ball possession and keep it for as long as possible. The ball can be covered by one's body.

Emphasis Training

Partner work with the gymnastics ball
- Partner A bounces the ball on the spot. Partner B trots around and with a sudden short spurt demands the ball. A immediately throws the ball to the running sprinter.
- Partner A has the ball by her foot. Player B trots around and suddenly spurts ahead. This is the signal for A to play the ball over to the sprinter on the run.
- Player A throws the ball straight up in the air. Both girls jump after the ball and try to catch it as it comes down.
- Player B bounces the ball down as hard as possible on the ground. Both jump after the ball and try to catch it.
- The players stand opposite each other at a distance of 3-4 m. A throws the ball up gently and plays it to her partner with her knee.
- Both players head the ball to each other. Then they both try and keep the ball up in the air together for as long as possible. This last exercise can also be carried out with all the partners at the same time in the form of a competition.

Putting it into Practice in a Game

Small games
Groups of seven are formed. Each group has a ball.
- They play six against one (6:1). The sixer team throws the ball to each other within a restricted area, moving in the process. The solo player has to try to touch the ball. In the second half the sixer team has to stand still and not move away from their positions. This makes it easier for the girl on her own. In this game the majority team have a lot of time for controlling the ball.
- The same game can then be played with the feet. A softball or volleyball can be used for beginners here.
- If the players are no longer beginners, it is possible to make the task more difficult by altering the ratio to 5:2.

Cool-down run

BF 2

BF 3

Getting in the mood/Warm-up

Games and exercises with the hoop
The hoops are laid out over a part of the pitch (e..g. 20 x 10m).
- The players all run around the hoops.
- On the next run they jump over each of the hoops.
- All players trot around freely. When they come to a hoop, they do a standing jump in and out of it.
- While trotting around, the players hop in and out of the hoop on one foot.
- The players run around and when the trainer gives a signal they sprint and stand in a hoop.
- While walking around, they balance their way once around each hoop they encounter.

The hoops are laid in a row, one behind the other.
- The players run around the hoops in a slalom.
- The players run around the hoops backwards in a slalom.
- The players jump from one hoop to the next.
- After a signal the players sprint to a hoop and stay standing in it on one leg.
- They stand in twos in a hoop, both on one leg, and try to portray a funny monument.

Emphasis Training

The Soccer can be used at last
Every girl has a Soccer ball.
- Take the ball in the hand, bounce it on the ground, kick it up in the air and catch it again. This exercise is done with both feet.
- The ball is dropped to the ground and is kicked up in the air several times by the foot before being caught again by the hands.
- The above exercise is repeated. This time the ball is only allowed to touch the ground once.
- Now it gets difficult, as this time the ball is not to touch the ground at all, but rather be kept up cleanly in the air.
- Which girl can keep the ball up in the air several times using her knee or head? Here too it is possible to start off with ground contact and then without.

Putting it into Practice in a Game

Games with the Soccer ball
On a section of the pitch (20 x 20m) six small goals are set up (1m) using traffic cones. The girls dribble on this area of the pitch and try to follow the trainer's instructions.

- Each girl dribbles as fast as possible through all the goals.
- This is done again. When a player is 5m in front of the goal, she then shoots the ball through the goal, sprints after it and continues dribbling to the next goal.
- Which player can shoot the most goals in 30 seconds? All play at the same time and and each girl counts for herself. One is allowed to shoot at the goal from both sides, but never the same goal twice in a row.
- To finish off there is a match with two small goals (1x1m) without a goal keeper. 4 play against 4 on an area of 20 x 15m.

Cool-down run

BF 4

Getting in the Mood/Warm-up

Games with a balloon
Each girl has a balloon.
- The balloon is balanced on the flat palm of the hand and should be kept lying there as long as possible.
- Pat the balloon up in the air with the flat palm of the hand, first to the right and then to the left.
- Now , keep the balloon up in the air with the foot, the knee or the head.
- The balloon is kicked up high and then headed upwards again. Who can manage this sequence three times in a row?
- The players throw the balloon through their straddled legs; they then turn round and catch it again.
- The balloon is kept up in the air using the shoulders and elbows.

Groups of four are formed; each group has four balloons.
- Each player keeps her balloon up in the air. On a signal the balloons are passed around to the next player.
- All four balloons are kept up in the air at the same time. Each girl is allowed only to tap the balloon up three times in a row.
- Three players have to keep the four balloons up in the air. The fourth player tries to disrupt them and knock a balloon down to the ground.

Emphasis Training

Once again the Soccer ball is used.
Each player has a Soccer ball.
First of all, two playing fields, both 20 x 15 m, are marked out beside each other. A 3m wide goal is set up in the middle between both playing fields using traffic cones.
- The players run with the ball close to their feet without touching the other players. On the trainer's signal the whole group changes over to the other field through the 3m wide goal. In the goal area a bottleneck occurs. The players have to watch out here as the dribbling changes from 'wide' to 'narrow'. The ball must be kept under control at all times.

- The changeovers continue in the two fields. One can add the following extra tasks to dribbling in the field: dribbling with tempo increases, dribbling with feint manoeuvres, dribbling with changes in direction.
- For the changeover of fields the following exercise must be done:
  The trainer gives a signal and the players have to shoot the ball through the goal from the position they are in at that moment. Then they must sprint quickly after the ball so that they have it under control again before it rolls out of the other field.

Putting it into Practice in a Game

Goal scoring games 1:1
The players form pairs together; each pair has a ball. 2m wide goals are set up, 10-15m apart.

- Each player shoots the ball at her opponent's goal, who in turn tries to save the ball.

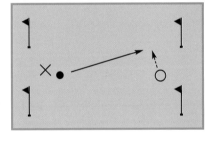

- A player dribbles towards the goal opposite and tries to get the ball into the goal. As soon as the other player gets hold of the ball it is now her turn to shoot at the other goal.

- The distance between the goals is reduced to 8-10m. The ball is now rolled and later thrown.

Cool-down run

BF 4

BF 5

Getting in the Mood/Warm-up

Skills circuit

On a circuit like this the players exercise their agility skills and coordination with and without the ball. The players complete a round with a Soccer ball and at certain stages carry out extra exercises. An area of about 40 x 40 m is required for this.

Nr. 1   Start
Nr. 2   Dribbling with the ball
Nr. 3   Throw the ball up five times and catch it with a leap.
Nr. 4   Dribbling around slalom poles.
Nr. 5   Jumping beside the ball; jumping on the ball with each leg alternately; standing jumps over the ball.

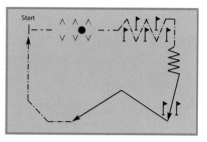

Nr. 6   Shooting through a goal (set up with traffic cones or flags) followed by a sprint after the ball.
Nr. 7   Kicking the ball up out of the hands, running after it and catching it.
Nr. 8   Dribbling with the left foot.

This circuit can be completed two or three times depending on the players' level of fitness.

Emphasis Training

Catching game without a ball

Catching games (game of tig) take place in a marked off section of the pitch, the size of which depends on the number of players. The penalty area is suitable in many cases.

- One player taps another who now takes over the catching role.
- Several catchers – about three in a training group – have to tig all the other players. Anyone who has been tigged goes into a crouched position and can be 'freed' again by another girl.
- Two catchers form the beginning of a chain. They try to tig other players who then have to join the chain. It is possible to tig from the front and the back of the chain.

- All players have a coloured ribbon hanging from the back of their trousers. A catcher now has to try to get hold of as many ribbons as possible within a set time. The game can be made more intensive by having two girls catching the ribbons at the same time.

As these running games are intensive and demanding, the girls take active breaks in between. Each girl plays around with a ball by herself for about three minutes to get her breath back.

Putting it into Practice in a Game

Winning the ball
The entire group is divided up into four teams. Each team takes up their position at a corner of a square (20 x 20 m). As many balls as possible are lying in the middle of the field.
- The trainer gives a sign and all players sprint to the middle, grab a ball and dribble back towards their corner. Which team is the first to be back in their corner?
- This game is repeated. However this time there is a different starting position. The players are lying on their backs and start when a sign is given. When standing up the girls' hands are not allowed to touch the ground.
- Different balls, are used at the next start; now tennis balls, rugby balls and other balls, difficult to control, are lying in the middle.
- On the way back from the middle, this time the ball is rolled with the hand.

Cool-down run

BF 5

BF 6

Getting in the mood/Warm-up

Coordination work with the ball
Each girl has a small ball e.g. a tennis ball in one hand, and in the other hand a large ball e.g. a gymnastics or volleyball.
- Both balls are balanced on the flat palm of the hand at the same time.
- First the big ball is bounced on the ground, then the small one is thrown up lightly in the air and caught again.
- The girls bounce both balls on the ground at the same time.
- They throw both balls up at the same time and catch them again.
- The players throw the small ball up and bounce the big ball down at the same time; this is done on the spot.
- Both balls are bounced onto the ground at the same time, then the girls do a full turn before catching them again.

Emphasis Training

Playing with a long rope
Two girls (not the same two the whole time) keep swinging the rope.
- The players run through the swinging rope without touching it at all.
- They enter the rope, jump about ten times and go out again.
- They run through the rope with partners.
- They enter the rope holding hands, jump a few times still holding hands and then go out.
- Chain-jumping: one girl is already jumping in the middle and another girl then joins her. They jump together a number of times. Then the first girl goes out and a new player jumps in.
- Two players are jumping in the middle, holding a ball between them.
- Two players stand opposite each other on either side of the rope, but outside of its radius, and throw the ball to each other through the rope.
- With the same starting position the girls now kick the ball to each other.
- The first exercises can be repeated when two ropes are swung within each other.

Putting it into Practice in a Game

Long shots – propelling the ball
The players form pairs; each pair has a ball between them.
- Each pair throws the ball to each other from as far away as possible. The partner has to throw it back from the place where she caught the ball.
- In the same game there is a bonus for catching the ball when it hasn't touched the ground. The catcher may take three steps forward before throwing the ball back.
- This time the girls shoot the ball to each other. The ball is kicked back from where it stopped rolling.
- When a shot can be stopped at the first attempt, the player may then lay the ball forward 5 metres before shooting back.
- The ball is kicked out of the hands this time, just like a goalkeeper.
- The game now takes the form of a throw-in.
- Finally one finishes up with a game of Soccer with all players using the entire pitch.

Cool-down run

BF 6

BF 7

Getting in the mood/Warm-up

Coordination exercises with the baton
Each player has a baton.
- The players balance the baton on the palms of their hands.
- They try the the same exerise, this time on the back of their hands.
- The baton is balanced on the index finger.
- The girls are in a bent position, holding the baton horizontally in one hand and they then jump over it.
- The baton is held on the ground in a vertical position and is then let go for an instant. At that moment the girls have to swing a leg over the baton and then take hold of it again.
- The baton is held in a vertical position and is then let go. After having done a full turn the player grasps hold of it again.
- A pair stands about 2m opposite each other. The baton is in a vertical position between both girls. The girl who is holding it suddenly lets go. The other girl must try and catch hold of it before it touches the ground. Deceptive moves are allowed!

Emphasis Training

Games with the ball
The entire team is divided up into two teams: Team A are the "runners" and Team B are the "passers". A playing area of 25 x 25 m is marked out.

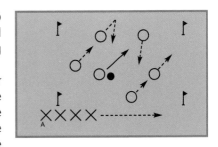

- Team A runs in relays (each player must run one round) around the square field area. Team B pass the ball to each other until A have finished their runs, counting the number of passes in the process. Then there is a changeover. Which team manages the most passes?
- Team B, on the field, throw the ball to each other.
- Team B players dribble with the ball close to their feet to the player opposite them.
- The ball is 'thrown-in' to the next player.

Putting it into Practice in a Game.

Ten-in-a-row handball/Soccer

Two teams are formed. A playing area of 25 x 20 m is marked out. Each team has to try and keep the ball in their possession for as long as possible. This means continuously running and looking for a pass. The opposing team on the other hand try to get ball possession as soon as possible.

- First of all the ball is thrown. Each 'successful' pass between players on the same side scores a point.
- The players now use their feet. If the ball is touched by a member of the other team then the scoring must begin again. Which team manages the greatest number of passes in one go?
- Finally, a game follows using two goals. The goals are as wide as the playing area i.e. 20 m.

Cool-down run

BF 7

BF 8

Coordination training with the ball
Each player has a ball.
- The players bounce the ball just as they like.
- While bouncing the ball there is a change in tempo and direction.
- The ball is bounced with the weak and strong hand alternately.
- The players dribble the ball freely.
- While dribbling the ball the trainer gives a signal and the players then juggle around with the ball in the air.
- The ball is moved forward using one knee in a spider's walk.
- In a supine position, with the ball pressed between the thighs, the players must roll to the right and the left.
- The girls are busy dribbling. When a sign is given they lift the ball up and then run around bouncing the ball for a time, throw the ball up in the air, block it with their feet and start dribbling again.

Improvement of coordination in relay form
The group is divided up into several relay teams and they line up as shuttle relays.
- Begin with slalom dribbling followed by a back pass. For the first part, a player dribbles her way through the slalom and passes the ball to the player opposite, who in turn plays the ball back to the opposite side with a long pass and then sprints after the ball.
- The ball is dribbled from both sides through the slalom, which this time has a lot of tricky bends.

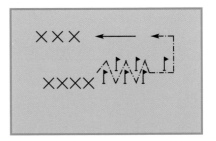

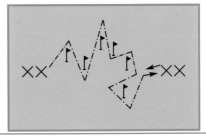

- For the first part a player passes the ball directly to the player opposite and then sprints after it. The player taking the pass now dribbles back through the slalom course.

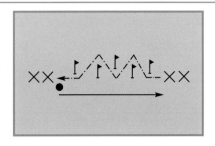

- To finish there is a one-way relay, starting off with slalom dribbling and ending up with a shot at goal.

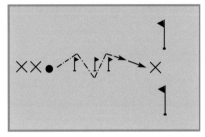

Putting it into Practice in a Game

Majority and minority games
- Two teams are formed with a ratio of 5:3. They play using two small goals and no goalkeeper. The game lasts five minutes with a starting score of 0:2. What's the final score?
- A second game takes place under the same conditions. While the players in the majority team are only allowed to use their weak foot, the minority team plays normally.

Cool-down run

BF 8

BF 9

Getting in the Mood/Warm-up

Skills circuit with stations

Pos. 1: Slalom dribbling.
Pos. 2: Throw the ball up with both hands and head it (ten attempts).
Pos. 3: Backwards dribbling, pulling the ball back with the sole of the foot.
Pos. 4: Juggle the ball, sending it up in the air as often as possible with and without ground contact.

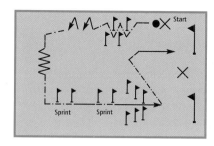

Pos. 5: Dribble the ball with the right and left foot alternately.
Pos. 6: Sprint with the ball and bring it to a stop; keep repeating this.
Pos. 7: Shoot the ball through a 'traffic cone alley' which gets narrower and narrower.
Pos. 8: Dribble the ball towards the goal and take a shot against the goalkeeper.

Emphasis Training

Playing the ball to each other accurately

The players form pairs. Both girls have a fixed spot, where they must remain standing.

- The players play the ball to each other accurately, receive it, bring it to a stop and pass it back again.
- The ball is thrown in so that the player can receive it with the body and then bring it to a stop with the foot. She then takes the ball in her hands and throws it back.
- The ball is passed directly i.e. it's not brought to a stop but passed back immediately.

From this point on the players are in motion

- The players run around passing the ball to each other with lows passes.
- The player without the ball always receives a pass when she changes her running direction.
- Both partners try to tackle the ball away from each other. Whoever is in ball possession, tries to protect the ball with her body.

- Both players have a ball and dribble along beside each other. During the first minute Player A carries out movements and exercises, which B has to follow and then the roles are swopped.
- The best pair may now select and suggest forms of movement and play for two minutes, which all the other pairs have to follow.

Putting it into Practice in a Game

Number competitions and games

Several teams are formed with a maximum of six players per team; each player gets a number. All players have a ball.

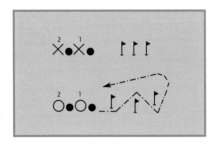

- The trainer calls out a number and each player with this number has to dribble one round of the slalom circuit.
- The trainer calls out a player's name from Team A who now has to dribble. The players standing parallel to her start at the same time too.
- The trainer claps a number and these players now have to run around the slalom circuit constantly bouncing the ball.
- To finish off with, teams of four play Soccer against each other with two small goals, without goalkeepers.

Cool-down run

BF 10

Getting in the Mood/Warm-up

Voelkerball
(A German game for two teams, where the object is to hit an opponent with a ball and thus put him out of the game). One can make it more interesting through a few variations.
- Two light balls (volleyball or softball) are used in the game. Every player who has been hit by the ball is a point for the other team. This is also the case when the ball hits the ground. But no player has to leave the field. At the end of the game one counts up each team's points.
- A medicine ball or another object of the same size is lying in the middle of each half of the field. If the opposite team manage to hit it, this scores ten points.
- Each team secretly picks out a player who is the 'hen in a basket'. The opposing team however doesn't know who this is. If this player is hit the game is lost.
- When playing Soccer-voelkerball the same rules apply as before. However if a team manages to shoot the ball through the entire length of the opponent's half without any contact, the team gains five extra points.

Emphasis Training

Ball dribbling and shooting techniques

Every player has a ball.
- The players dribble around a slalom circuit and finally shoot the ball through a small goal marked by flags.
- They dribble through the slalom circuit and try to hit one of three traffic cones with a shot.
- After dribbling through a slalom lane the players shoot at the goal where a goalkeeper is standing waiting.
- The ball is passed between pairs and the passing finishes up with a shot at goal with a goalkeeper there.

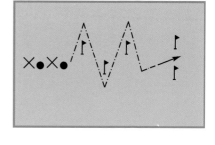

Putting it into Practice in a Game

Shots at goal and little games
Several gymnastic hoops are hung up in a goal at various heights.
- Which player manages to shoot through the hoops the most with five shots?
- Pairs are formed. Each player has five shots. How many shots does a pair need in order to shoot through all the hoops?
- Two teams play Soccer at hoops, which represent the goal. Each shot through a hoop counts as a goal. Which team wins?

Cool-down run

8.2 Dribbling – Ball Control – Ten Training Sessions

One very soon sees the connection between the theme of "Dribbling-Ball Control" and the previous theme "Ball Familiarisation". However, from the content point of view new territory is broken here, which requires the players to be able to work well with a ball beforehand. This shows that the five theme areas have many common factors and intertwine with each other.

Being able to control and dribble the ball means that the players have to be already familiar with the ball in the first place. The central point here is working with other team members as well as ball control, even when under attack from the opponents, which means a realistic training structure is possible. For successful training, realistic play must always be considered.

DB 1

Getting in the Mood/Warm-up

Controlling the Ball
All players have a ball each.
- Each girl runs with the ball close to her feet on a marked out area of the field. Other players do not interupt or get involved.
- Sudden changes in direction mean that the players have to react or make evasive manoeuvres.
- Dribbling speeds up gradually to become a short sprint.
- Dribbling tempo changes constantly.
- When the trainer gives a signal, the players stop the ball with the sole of the foot and pull it back. They continue dribbling in the opposite direction.
- While trotting, the ball is kicked up to face height and then brought to a stop again with the sole of the foot.
- Which girl is brave enough to risk an overhead kick?
- The ball is kicked up out of the hands as far and straight as possible. When it drops back down again it is stopped with the foot.

Emphasis Training

Dribbling and Pass Combinations

Ball control and dribbling in a match are always combined with a pass to another player. For this reason, pairs are formed with one ball between the two of them.

- The players move around freely in a marked off area of the pitch and pass the ball to each other.
- The ball should be passed in such a way that the partner neither has to reduce or increase her running speed.
- While dribbling with the ball, the players must always keep an eye on their partners so that the ball can be passed at exactly the right moment.
- While playing with the partner, some passing deception manoeuvres are made.
- The player with ball possession changes the direction she's running in before passing to her partner; thus the partner has to keep a constant eye on her in order to be able to follow these changes of direction.
- On a marked out area, numerous traffic cones are set up as obstacles, which hinder the partners' ball passing.
- When passing between each other, the girls lob semi-high balls over the traffic cones.

Putting it into Practice in a Game

Dribbling with a Shot at Goal

- Coming from various starting positions, the players dribble towards a manned goal and take a shot.
- When dribbling towards the goal, each player has three attempts at a shot with the strong and with the weak foot.
- The ball is played forward; the player does a forward tumble, then sprints after the ball and takes a shot at goal.
- The trainer plays the ball in the direction of the goal. The player makes a spurt after it and takes a shot at goal.
- Two players pass the ball to each other. At the penalty line one player takes a low shot at the goal.
- Finally, pairs are formed who then play against each other defending a small goal.

Cool-down run

DB 2

Getting in the Mood/Warm-up

Dribbling with changes in tempo and direction
Each player has a ball.
- The players dribble with the ball in a prescribed area. They try to incorporate little tricks and artistic elements in the process.
- Dribbling now takes place with the weak foot.
- While dribbling the tempo is increased and reduced.
- The players lie down with their arms stretched out in front. They raise their upper body with their hands still outstretched.
- Sitting cross-legged and soles touching each other, the knees are pressed downwards with the elbows.
- Stopping the dribble: each player dribbles with her ball and another player tries to take the ball away. The ball must be kept close to the foot.
- Two field areas (10 x 10 m) are marked out with 20m between them. Half of the entire team is dribbling in each field. On a signal from the trainer, both teams change over to the other field. A four metre-wide goal is set up in the middle between the two fields to make things a little more difficult as all players have to dribble through it.

Emphasis Training

Ball control at station points
Aim is the improvement of technical skills at the playing points. 4-5 players can practise at each station for 5-8 minutes.

Station 1: Dribbling through a forest of traffic cones, followed by a shot at goal.
Station 2: Ball juggling using both feet, thighs and knees.
Station 3: Two-a-side game with two small goals.
Station 4: Passing high balls over long distances.
Station 5: Two-a-side game with one small goal.

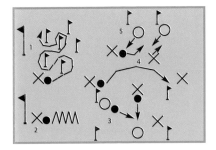

Putting it into Practice in a Game

After the players have worked on improving their technical skills in the emphasis training phase, it's now time to apply it to a game situation. Therefore a four-a-side tournament is played. Goals count as in a normal match. However if a player scores a goal, having 'dribbled' round past one or more of her opponents, the score is doubled.

Cool-down run

DB 2

DB 3

Getting in the Mood/Warm-up

Dribbling in the form of games and competition
Each player has a ball.
- The players play with the ball in an open area.
- Various types of obstacles are set up in a marked out area, where the players have to dribble around them.
- Stretching exercises: In a standing position with a straight back and straddled legs, one bends the left leg until one clearly senses a pulling feeling in the right inner thigh. The hands are placed on the hips and the exercise is repeated three times on each side.
- Stretching exercises: Lying on the back, grasp a bent knee and pull it toward the chest three times.

- Two teams are formed. The participants of both teams stand 2-3m opposite each other. When the trainer calls out "A" then the members of Team A dribble with the ball towards the B team members opposite them – who are also busy dribbling – as far as a certain line. Then Team B has a go.

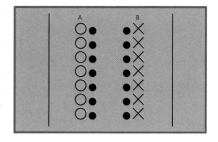

- The same game can be played with different starting positions (prone position, supine position, on all fours etc).

Emphasis Training

Dribbling and passing combinations in groups of three
Small 1 m goals are set up in a prescribed playing area.
- When practising passing in groups of three, the goals count as an obstacle and the players have to play around them. First the ball is brought to a stop, then dribbled and played on again. Later on the ball is to be passed directly.
- Now the players have to play the ball through the goals, although playing through the same goal twice in a row is not allowed.

- The player running with the ball kicks it up into her hands, throws it up and heads it to B: Player B takes it with her foot and passes the ball to C.
- Which team requires the least amount of time to play the ball through all the goals?

Putting it into Practice in a Game

Dribbling, passing combinations, shots at goal
The activity tasks in the emphasis training phase are now completed with shots at goal.
- The groups of three pass the ball to each other again. The trainer calls one player by her name. Her group carries out passing combinations towards the goal, ending off with a shot at goal against the goalkeeper.
- The group called out approaches the goal, dribbling and passing. As soon as they have entered the penalty area the player with the ball tries to score a goal from 5m. The two other players, however, try to prevent this, by then playing defender from the penalty area onwards.

Cool-down run

DB 4

Getting in the Mood/Warm-up

Dribbling relays and little games
Relays and little games enhance ball control under pressure – time and opponent. As well as this they are a lot of fun and are directed towards the competitive character of the game of Soccer. Each player has a ball. Two playing fields (10 x 10 m) are marked out situated about 20m apart from each other.

- All players except one are dribbling in field A. The player on her own is running in field B with no ball. On the trainer's signal all players change over to the other field. As this is going on the player on her own fights to get the ball from another girl. If she succeeds then it's another girl's turn on her own in the field.

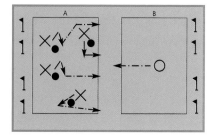

- Instead of dribbling one can also start off with juggling or heading. During the changeover however the players dribble.
- The players are divided equally on both fields. The players in field A have one ball each and have to dribble across to field B, which the B players try to prevent.

Emphasis Training

Taking the ball away from a dribbling player in a game
- The girls play 1:1 on a playing field of 10 x 10 m with two small 1 m goals. After playing for three minutes the two opponents join to form a team and play 2:2 against another team, again for three minutes.
- The next round is a 4:4 game lasting five minutes, but before this the playing field is extended to 20 m x 15 m.
- When this round is completed, another two rounds follow, this time 2:2 and 1:1, again lasting three minutes each.
- As these games are very intensive and demanding, an activity break is necessary after each round. This can take the form of two players passing the ball to each other or each girl playing with the ball by herself.

Putting it into Practice in a Game

Majority and minority games
The game is played with two goals, with or without a goalkeeper depending on the size of the teams. Particular activities are assigned to each game.

- The first game is played 4:2 with a goalkeeper. The majority team have to take a shot at goal after five passes.
- When playing 2:1 with small goals and without a goalkeeper, each member of the majority team is only allowed to have contact with the ball twice.
- When playing 5:2 with a goalkeeper, the minority team are also allowed to play the ball with their hands (as in handball). The majority team are allowed, on the other hand, to win the ball back with their hands but are only allowed to kick the ball when playing.

Cool-down run

DB 5

Getting in the Mood/Warm-up

Dribbling and bouncing

Improving the girls' management of the ball and coordination should occur in a play form. Each player has a ball. The trainer gives the following things to be carried out.

- The players dribble around in an open space keeping the ball very close.
- The players dribble in an open space with the strong and the weak foot alternately.
- The players juggle the ball in the air.
- The players bounce the ball while hopping on one leg.
- All players bounce the ball in a prescribed area of the field. On hearing the trainer's signal, each player tries to kick another player's ball away without losing her own.
- While dribbling around with the ball a player tries to disrupt another player's dribbling and kick it away.

Emphasis Training

Station work with partners

Two players, with a ball each, complete seven station points using it.

- Station 1
  The ball is passed in an easy trot. Each player may only have contact with the ball twice (receive and pass back).
- Station 2
  Both partners run across the field doing throw-ins.
- Station 3
  Partner A throws-in to B, who stops the ball with her foot, dribbles along for a few metres and then kicks the ball up gently into A's hands again.
- Station 4
  Two goals are situated opposite each other 10 m apart. Both players keep on taking shots at the opposing goal. Who scores the most goals?
- Station 5
  Shadow dribbling with a few built-in 'artistic' elements, which player A performs and B has to follow. Then roles are swopped.

- Station 6
  Two goals are set up 6 m from each other. Both players are in the goals and try to score goals by heading. The ball is thrown up and then headed towards the opponent's goal.
- Station 7
  The players play 1:1 with small goals.

Putting it into Practice in a Game

Game in small groups
- Two 1 m goals are set up on each of the longer sides of a small playing field (20 x 15m). Now two three-a-side teams play against each other and have the opportunity to score in both goals.
- Two four-a-side teams play on the small playing area; the game situation changes after each goal. The player who scores the goal changes to the other team so that a 3:5 ratio exists.

Cool-down run

DB 5

DB 6

Getting in the Mood/Warm-up

Dribbling with tempo changes
Each player has a ball.
- The players dribble with the ball in the centre circle and are not allowed to leave this circle.
- When dribbling in the centre circle the ball is kicked up a little when crossing the centre line.
- Stretching exercises: With a lunge step, place the left knee on the ground, and bend down with the back straight until tension can be felt at the hip and in the thigh. This exercise is repeated three times and held for about ten seconds.
- Stretching exercises: With the back straight and the pelvis in a locked position, pull the lower leg up to the bottom.
- The following activities have to be completed in each corner of a square:

Corner 1
The trainer calls out names and these girls dribble with the ball. One player tries to get the ball away from them.
Corner 2
Other players are dribbling here, and they have to keep an eye on the trainer all the time. If she raises her arm then they must bring the ball to a stop immediately.
Corner 3
The ball is juggled in the air for as long as possible. Each player has three attempts.
Corner 4
The ball is driven forward with the outside of the foot and still has to stay close to the foot.

Emphasis Training

Dribbling and shots at goal in pairs
Pairs are formed, each with a ball between them.
- Two players pass the ball to each other from the centre line onwards and take a shot at goal from the edge of the penalty area. The goalkeeper is in the goal.

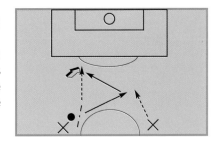

- Player A dribbles the ball from the centre line towards the goal. At the edge of the penalty area she passes to Player B who has run along parallel with her. Player B now takes a shot at the goal.
- Player B dribbles from the side-line towards the goal and plays a cross-pass in front of the goal. Player A, who has followed up, takes a shot at goal to finish.
- Player A kicks a high ball from the centre line towards the goal. Player B sprints after the ball and takes a shot at goal to finish.
- Both players sprint from the centre line towards the goal and try to get to the ball which is lying on the edge of the penalty area. The winner takes a shot at goal.

Putting it into Practice in a Game

Soccer tennis

The playing areas necessary for this are marked out with traffic cones. A string is tied up in the middle between the two areas (tied onto two movable goals).

- In the first round the ball is allowed to touch the ground twice. In the second round only once.
- In the third round the ball is allowed to touch the ground once, but there are double points for successful headers.

Cool-down run

DB 6

DB 7

Getting in the Mood/Warm-up

Games with a balloon
Each player has a balloon.
- The balloon is kept up in the air with the head and shoulders.
- The balloon is kept up in the air using the back of the hand and elbow.
- Thigh and knee keep the balloon up.
- The balloon is kept up alternately with the right and left foot.
- Stretching exercises: Lying in the prone position, the forehead is leaning on the back of the hand. Keeping the back straight one pulls the lower leg up to the bottom three times.
- Stretching exercises: Lying on the back, lean forward, take hold of the shins and pull the knees towards the forehead.
- The balloon is tapped up in the air with the feet. Before it lands on the floor again the player does a forward roll and kicks the balloon up again.
- Moving along with the balloon balanced in their hand, each player tries to hit another player's balloon away.

Emphasis Training

Dribbling and passing using the inside of the foot
Groups of five are formed; each group has a ball.
- The players pass the ball to each other freely and in random order.
- While playing free passing, a player's sudden forward movement is the signal to pass the ball to her.
- The ball is passed to a player who in turn passes it directly back again.
- While passing to each other, each player is only allowed to touch the ball twice.
- The group of five elect a 'trouble-maker'. This player tries to hinder the other four players when passing to each other.
- A game is played on a small field (10 x 10 m) with 3:2. At one end is a 2 m wide goal, against which the majority team play. The minority team can use the full width of the other end as a goal.

Putting it into Practice in a Game

Ball control in a game
A small four-a-side tournament is played, which has particular rules. Playing time is five minutes in each case.

- The ball is passed around inside a limited playing area. If a team manages to pass the ball to each other six times in a row without the opponents getting at it, they earn a point.
- This time one player has to dribble with the ball for as long as possible before passing it. If a player manages to cover a dribbling distance of ten metres in one go her team earns a point.
- Each team has to try and make as many passes in a row as possible. However, these passes to the other players must be high. Which team succeeds in getting the longest passing chain in the time allowed for the game?

Cool-Down run

DB 7

DB 8

Gymnastics and games with the baton
Each player has a baton.
- The baton is balanced on the right or the left palm of the hand.
- The baton is balanced vertically on the foot.
- Stretching exercise: The baton is held up above above the head and moved to the right or the left.
- Stretching exercise: As above, but this time one bends to the side when moving the baton.
- Holding the baton straight out in front, raise the right or the left knee up towards it.
- The baton is placed standing up, and the right and left leg is passed over it alternately.
- Two partners take a baton between them. The third player sits on the baton and is carried around.
- Two players walk behind each other, holding the end of a baton in both hands. A third player stands up on the two batons and is carried around, holding onto the shoulder of the player in front.

Parallel technique training
Two teams of the same size are formed.

On one half of the pitch Team 1 and Team 2 play against each other using two small goals without a goalkeeper. The size of the playing area depends on the number of players.

On the other half of the pitch two exercises are carried out.

- A player dribbles towards a manned goal and takes a shot from about the penalty line (Team 3)
- A player dribbles parallel to the penalty area and takes a shot at goal from the turn (Team 4).

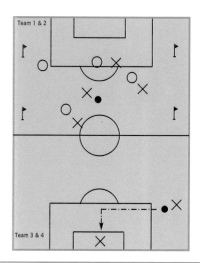

Putting it into Practice in a Game

Game and endurance dribbling
Two teams are formed who now play with two goals including a goalkeeper.

- Two players of each team are not in the game from the start. Instead they dribble all the way round the playing field. The player is relieved from dribbling around the field when a player takes a shot at the goal.
- While Team A plays with a full team, two members of Team B do rounds of dribbling. When the first goal is scored, by whatever team, the dribblers from Team B now enter the game and two players from Team A take over the dribbling.

Cool-Down run

DB 9

Getting in the Mood/Warm-up

Improving running coordination: games with the hoop
Each girl has a hoop.
- The hoops are laid down in a row and the players run through the row of hoops several times.
- The players run a slalom through the hoops.
- The players hop through the hoops on the strong foot, then the weak foot and finally with both legs.
- The players run a slalom through the hoops, stepping into only every second hoop.
- Every second hoop is pushed about one metre to the right. The players run through the circuit again. Running with a steady rhythm, the first step lands in a hoop and the next step outside.
- In order to work on running coordination the hoops are placed wider apart from each other. One step is in the hoop and the next two steps occur outside.
- The hoops are laid out randomly across the field. The players have to run through them as evenly and steadily as possible.

Emphasis Training

Dribbling with a shot at goal
Dribbling and ball control should end up with a shot at goal as often as possible. Each player works with a ball.
- The players start off dribbling from the centre line and, at the edge of the penalty area, take a shot at goal.
- The players start off dribbling from the right or left side-line towards the goal and take a shot at goal from the edge of the penalty area.
- The players dribble towards the goal and, at the edge of the penalty area an opposing player is waiting, who tries to win the ball using 70% effort. The player with the ball forces her way into the penalty area where she may no longer be attacked, and finishes off the action with a shot at goal.
- A slalom lane is set up between the halfway line and the edge of the penalty area. The ball is accurately shot past the slalom lane; at the same time the player runs through the slalom lane and gathers the ball up at the other end and takes a shot at goal.

- Three balls are used here, each of which is kicked back out onto the field again by the goalkeeper when a shot has been taken. The players gather up the balls, dribble up to the edge of the penalty area and take another shot at goal.

Putting it into Practice in a Game

Three-Zone game
The pitch is divided up into three areas. Only certain players are allowed to enter the different zones. The trainer can use the following game play:
Field 1
Three defending players: two attackers
Field 2
3:3 in the middle area
Field 3
Two attackers: three defenders

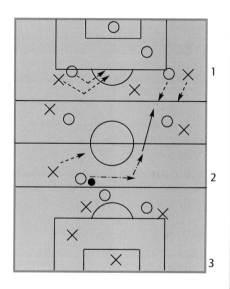

Cool-down run

DB 10

Getting in the Mood/Warm-up

A newspaper helps when warming up
Each player has a newspaper which is used when warming up.
- The players take the newspaper in both hands and run around holding it above their head like a fluttering flag.
- The players now hold it to the side, and run round a figure of eight, a circle or other shapes.
- The newspaper is lying on the ground. The girls hop around it first with their left, and then with their right foot.
- They jump over the paper with both feet, forwards, backwards and sidewards.
- Stretching exercises: they lie on the newspaper, stomach down, keeping their back straight and leaning their forehead on the back of their hand. With the other hand they pull the lower leg to their bottom.
- Stretching exercises: standing in a lunge step, the girls lay their left knee on the ground and bend down with their back straight until they can feel a slight pull in their thighs and hips.
- The players roll the newspaper into a stick and grasp it at both ends. Then they jump over it.
- The newspaper is folded up several times. The players have to stand on one leg on the small space of the folded paper. Any player who loses her balance has to start off again with the newspaper unfolded.

Emphasis Training

Dribbling and shooting
Each player has a ball.
- The ball is bounced with the right hand, thrown forward and the player must then sprint after it. The ball is brought under control and then dribbling is resumed, ending up with an aimed shot at an object (sports bag, ball etc).
- The players bounce the ball along for several metres with the right hand, then the left. The player then throws the ball to the rear and she turns round and sprints after it. As soon as the ball is under control again, a shot is taken at a 1 metre wide goal from a distance of 15 m.
- The ball is headed forward. As it falls to the ground, it is quickly brought under control and the player immediately takes a shot at an obstacle.

- A slalom circuit is set up, leading towards the goal, using several flag poles; all the players have to run through this slalom. At the end, a ball is passed to her on the move. She uses this ball to take a direct shot at goal.
- The players shoot the ball past the slalom course and then sprint after it through the 'forest of flags'. When a player catches up with her ball, she takes a shot at goal using her weak foot.

Putting it into Practice in a Game

The winners change over

A 2:2 game is played with two small goals and no goalkeeper. The pitch is divided into four sectors. Playing time is two minutes in each case. The winning team change over to the playing field on the left, the losing team stay where they are. After each changeover a new game is played. Which team manages a changeover in all games?

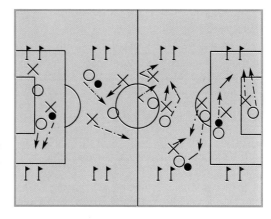

Cool-down run

8.3 Shooting Techniques –
Ways of Delivery – Ten Training Sessions

The description of the various shooting techniques is determined by the part of the foot that comes into contact with the ball. Reducing this down to a particularly important criterium serves as a starting point for the various ways of delivery. In his book "Soccer. Technique & Tactics", Erich LOLLATH refers to five sub-divisions of shooting techniques.

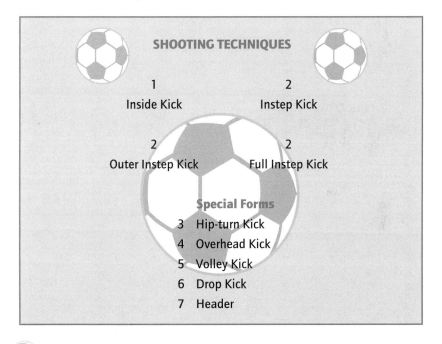

SHOOTING TECHNIQUES

| 1 | 2 |
| Inside Kick | Instep Kick |

| 2 | 2 |
| Outer Instep Kick | Full Instep Kick |

Special Forms

3 Hip-turn Kick
4 Overhead Kick
5 Volley Kick
6 Drop Kick
7 Header

1 Inside Kick

The ball is played with the inside of the foot. Short passes are used with this shooting technique; one can judge the right amount of speed, strength etc. and it allows a considerably accurate shot.

Criteria
- Standing leg is next to the ball.
- Playing the ball with the inside of the foot.
- Upper body above the ball.

2 Instep kick (Inner, outer, full)

The ball is played using the instep. This is good for passes over a long distance, such as centre cross passes, corners and goal shots. Besides this, it is possible to hook the ball e.g. a player can turn a free kick around the wall of defence.

Criteria
- The player approaches the ball from an angle.
- Standing leg is next to the ball.
- The tip of the playing foot is pointing at the ground.
- The ball is played with either the inner, outer or full instep.
- The direction and spin on the ball determine the ball's target zone.

3 Hip-turn kick

The ball is passed sideways at hip level.

Criteria
- Initial rotation around the body's longitudinal axis.
- The standing leg is bent.
- The ball is played with the instep sideways beside the body at hip level.

4 Overhead kick (also called the bicycle kick)

Overhead kicks come into use when it is necessary to get the ball out of the way quickly or when a high approaching ball enables a surprise attack on the goal.

Criteria
- The initial phase takes the form of a scissors-kick.
- The ball is kicked above head level.
- The body is in a horizontal position.

5 Volley kick

Volley shots come as a surprise in a match as the ball is kicked out of the air directly. Such a situation arises when taking a shot at goal or when a defender has to clear the ball back down the field.

Criteria
- The ball is kicked on directly.
- One specifically kicks the ball in a particular direction.
- The technique is the same as for a full instep kick.

6 Drop Kick

The Ball is bounced in front of the player, who kicks it as a drop kick. This shooting technique enables the players to take a fast, hard shot.

Criteria
- The standing leg is bent.
- The tip of the foot of the standing leg is pointing in the direction of the kick.
- The ball is kicked immediately after it touches the ground.
- The shot takes place with the instep or inside of the foot next to the standing leg.
- The leg follows through with the kick.

7 Header

The header is used against high balls.

Criteria
- The ball is hit with the forehead.
- Tense the neck and trunk muscles up.
- Go up to the ball with the head.

ST 1

Getting in the Mood/Warm-up

Coordination and stretching exercises

The following stretching exercises enhance ball skills and improve coordination. They serve as a guideline for a stretching programme and can be built on as required.

Each player has a ball.

- The players throw the ball up, touch the ground briefly with both hands and catch the ball again.
- Sitting on the ground with their legs out, the players throw the ball up, stand up quickly and catch the ball.
- After throwing the ball up the players roll over once before catching the ball.
- The ball is thrown up, the players go into a crouch position briefly and jump up to catch the ball.
- Lying on the back, one leg is stretched, the other is bent. The players grasp the knee of the bent leg and pull it towards their chest.
- Starting off in a straddle position with the upper body erect, the weight is placed on the leg that is bent.
- Bouncing the ball when running.
- Moving the ball with the foot while on the move. The ball is lobbed up into the hands at regular intervals.
- Starting off in a stride position on all fours, with a straight upper body and the pelvis tilted forward, stretch the hip joint.
- Lying on the back, the player rolls into a ball, pulling the knees in towards the chest.
- The players trot around gently with the ball and keep on trying to incorporate some ball-tricks.

Emphasis Training

Passing combination using the inside of the foot

Two players train with a ball between them.

- The players stand opposite each other and pass the ball to each other. They receive the ball cleanly before passing it back.
- The players now pass the ball directly to each other. The ball should be passed as accurately and cleanly as possible.

- The two exercises above are now carried out on the move.
- The pairs run beside each other, with a little gap between them. Each player dribbles a short distance before passing it to her partner. The ball should be passed in such a way that the partner has to neither sprint nor stop the ball in order to take it .

Putting it into Practice in a Game

Passing relays and a match with two goals

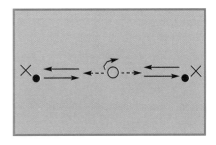

Groups of three are formed, each group has two balls between them. The two outside Players 1 and 2 receive a ball each. The midfield Player 3 receives passes from 1 and 2 alternately. Each time she runs towards the ball, passes the ball back and turns around to take the pass from her other neighbour.

- Now the ball taken by the player in the middle is passed on to another outside player, who at the same time has to pass her ball to the midfield player.
- The groups of three now go on to play a match using two small goals. All teams play against each other until each team has won at least two matches. Playing time is three minutes in each case.

Cool-down run

ST 2

Games and exercises with a skipping rope

Every player has a skipping rope.
- The players skip on the spot.
- All players skip around in a prescribed area.
- The players fold the rope double, hold it over their head and move it back as far as possible.
- Holding the rope with outstretched arms over their heads, the girls move it to the right and then the left.
- In the same position twist the trunk round in both directions.
- The rope is held in one hand and swung round in a circle; the girls jump over it.
- A pair stands beside each other holding their inside hands. They then skip by swinging the rope with their outside hands, forwards and backwards.
- The rope is folded double and held firm at both ends.The players bring their left and right knee up to it alternately.
- Finally, the players may invent their own exercises or games with the skipping rope.

Target shots at goal using the inside of the foot

Each player has a ball.
- The players dribble round freely, with changes in tempo and direction.
- Several small goals (1 m wide) are set up on the playing field. The players dribble round with the ball. Using the inside of their foot they take a shot at each goal from about 5 m.
- The previous exercise is now carried out further away from the goal.
- Which player manages a successful round of shots at every goal when striking from 10 m away?
- Hoops or rings are hanging in the goal, albeit quite close to the ground. Now the players have to score goals using the inside of their foot.
- In a 1:1 game using a small goal, the players are only allowed to dribble with the inside of their foot. Using the wrong side results in the opponent getting ball possession. Each player confesses her own mistakes.
- Five rings are hanging in the goal, each player has five attempts. Who manages to shoot through all five rings in one go?

Putting it into Practice in a Game

Match using two goals and 'out-of-bounds' zones

- An 'out-of-bounds' zone is marked out in the centre of the playing field. The players are not allowed to enter this area with the ball, and are therefore forced to pass the ball in order to get round this hurdle. The Game is played in teams of four.
- The out-of-bounds zone has a different role now. This time the ball is not allowed to enter it at all. The team in ball possession must get round this area with a long pass.

Cool-down run

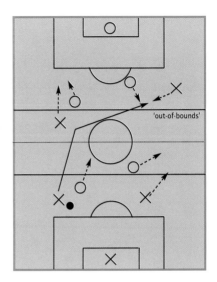

'out-of-bounds'

ST 3

Getting in the Mood/Warm-up

Games with the gymnastic hoop
The gymnastics hoop is very popular with girls. It can help to improve fitness and coordination. Each player works with a gymnastic hoop.
- The players roll the hoop along beside them.
- Each girl rolls her hoop forward from a standing position and then has to sprint after it to catch it again.
- The hoop is rolled forward from the standing position and the girls run to overtake it.
- The hoop is thrown out in front in such a way that it comes rolling back again.
- The hoop is held in front like a steering wheel and turned to and fro.
- The girls hold the hoop up vertically and then bend over to both sides.
- The players stand in the hoop holding it with both hands. The hoop is then turned as far as possible to the left and to the right.
- The girls bring the hoop down from the head to the toes and climb out of it again.
- The hoop is placed standing on the floor and is spun around like a spinning top. The girl now hops once round the spinning hoop on one leg.
- Two players place their hoops on top of each other and hold on to both at one end. A tug-of-war begins. Who can pull their teammate out of position?
- The player rolls her hoop, overtakes it in a sprint and finally makes a straddle jump over the approaching hoop.

Emphasis Training

Instep kick
The players form pairs together. Each pair has a ball. The ball is passed using the instep.
- The ball is passed over long distances.
- The ball is passed on the move using the instep.
- The players dribble along the edge of the penalty area parallel to the goal and take a shot at the goal from a turning position.
- The player kicks the ball ahead, spurts after it and then takes a shot with the instep.
- Pairs play around with the ball using their instep. The ball is kicked back from exactly where the player gathered the ball.
- One partner dribbles along the side-line as far as the goal line and centres from this position into the front of the goal. The other player who is waiting round the penalty sport converts this pass with an instep kick.

Putting it into Practice in a Game

Match with 'out-of-bounds' zones
The 'out-of-bounds' zones force the players to make long passes with the ball using the instep. In Field A and Field C, a goalkeeper and two defenders play against three attackers; no player is allowed to enter Field B. The players have to play over Field B using instep kicks.

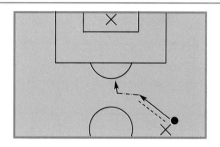

The 'out-of-bounds' zones are now the side-line areas. Only the attackers are allowed to enter this area. Defenders are not allowed to play here. In this way the attackers have time to give good centre-passes in front of the goal. A goal following a centre earns double points.

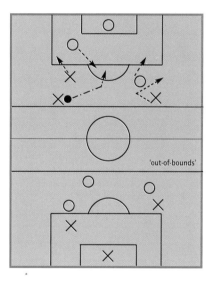

'out-of-bounds'

Cool-down run

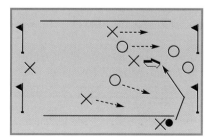

ST 3

ST 4

Getting in the Mood/Warm-up

Games with balloons and soccer balls
The aim here is to improve coordination and ball skills. Each participant requires a balloon and a Soccer ball.
- The players bounce the ball on the ground and hold the balloon up with the other hand.
- The ball is held in both hands and using it, the balloon is kept up in the air.
- Ball and balloon are placed one on each palm and balanced at the same time.
- The players stand on one leg. The other leg is placed on the ball on the ground. They hit the balloon to and fro above their head with both hands.
- Stretching exercise: a player stands on one leg, pulls her other foot towards her bottom, thus stretching the hips.
- Stretching exercise: the players sit cross-legged with the soles of the feet touching each other. Using both elbows, push the knees down to the ground.
- Stretching exercise: in the straddle position, grip the neck with both hands and pull the head forward gently.
- Keeping it close to the feet the players dribble with the ball, at the same time throwing the balloon up in the air and catching it again.
- The players dribble with their weak foot and keep the balloon up in the air with their head.

Emphasis Training

Drop kick
Each player has a ball.
- While dribbling round freely, the girls include changes in direction and tempo as well as stopping exercises.
- The players take the ball in their hand, let it drop to the ground, and shoot it away using their full instep. They sprint after it, dribble with the ball, kick it up into their hands and begin again.
- Passing in partners: A throws the ball to B in such a way that B can kick it back with a drop kick. The throw is best done with an underarm lob.
- Two goals are set up, about 15 m apart from each other. A player is standing in each goal. Player A sends the ball high to B, who then tries to score a goal with a drop kick.

- The two players stand at each end in goal. Player A drops the ball out of her hands onto the ground and takes a drop kick shot against the opposite goal. Player B has to hold this shot and reply with a drop kick. Who scores the most goals out of ten shots?

Putting it into Practice in a Game

Game with several goals

Playing with several goals improves the players' tactical understanding of the game. This is where they learn terms such as the marking of players and areas, and get an overall view of the game in practice. They can then react within their team through agreed arrangements, shouts to each other and being allocated specific tasks.

- On a large playing area, a 4:4 game is played with four goals. Two goals are placed an each short side. Each team must now defend two goals but can also attack two goals.

- This game can be played again with a goal on each side of the playing field. Each team can attack three goals (one goal on the short side and two goals on the long sides), but also have to defend three goals. Quick thinking is required by all players.

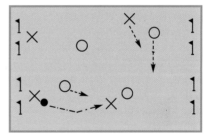

Cool-Down run

ST 4

ST 5

Getting in the Mood/Warm-up

Games in groups of three

Many competitive elements can be learned and trained with groups of three. The basic 2:1 situation means that both attackers have to be able to run freely, pass well, have good ball control and a good eye for the game; the defender must be able to position herself skilfully in play, attack at the right moment and have good ball control under increased pressure from her opponents.

- The players pass the ball to each other at an easy trot.
- Passing tempo is increased.
- The passing distances are increased; passing must remain accurate however.
- Stretching exercise: The players lie on the ground on their backs; put their arms around one knee and pull it to their chest.
- Stretching exercise: The players lie on their back, their arms are stretched out to the side. One leg is flexed and placed across the other leg, the head turns in the other direction.
- A 2:1 game is played on a marked out area against a small goal, without a goalkeeper.
- After that a 2:1 game is played using two small goals.
- During the 2:1 game the two attackers can only take a shot at goal after three passes to each other.

Emphasis Training

Shots at goal from various positions

Each player has a ball.

- The players dribble diagonally towards the goal and finish off the attack with a shot at goal. This exercise is carried out from both sides.
- The players kick the ball up ahead of them with such precision that they can catch up with it at the edge of the penalty area and take a shot at goal from there.

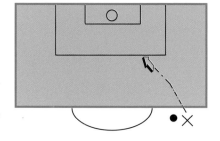

- On the way to the goal the ball is passed to the trainer who is standing on the edge of the penalty area. She in turn passes the ball back enabling the player to take a shot at goal. This exercise is carried out with passes from both sides.

Putting it into Practice in a Game

Goal scoring competitions
- Who scores the most goals in five shots?

Version·1

Version 2

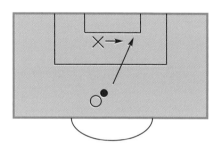

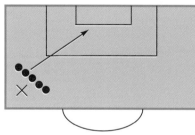

Version 3

- In the third version a ball is kicked from the left and the right alternately. A maximum of 2 minutes playing time is given.

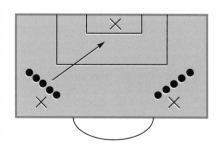

Hint: When playing goal-shooting games, change the goalkeeper often. All players have the opportunity to stand in goal and take a shot at it.

Cool-Down run

ST 5

ST 6

Getting in the Mood/Warm-up

Throwing and passing with a partner
The girls form pairs. Each pair has a ball.
- The ball is passed to the partner using the inner/outer instep.
- The player trots along, kicks the ball up into her hands and throws it to her partner who catches the ball and dribbles with it for a few metres before kicking it up into her hands and throwing it back again.
- The player trots along and throws the ball to her partner, who this time has to bring it to a stop with her foot in such a way that it doesn't bounce away from her.

Both players stand about 8-10 m opposite each other.
- The ball is thrown in and then brought to a stop using the foot.
- The ball is thrown in, this time with a bounce and the partner passes it back immediately.
- The ball is thrown backwards between one's legs to the partner who has to bring it to a stop.
- The ball is thrown up lightly and headed to the partner.
- Stretching exercise: In a wide straddled position with a straight back, the players bend the left/right leg until tension can be clearly felt in the other thigh. The arms are placed on the hips.
- Stretching exercise: In a stride position bring the left knee down onto the ground. Lean the upper-body forwards keeping the back straight and then lift back up again.
- Arms and legs are loosened up.

Emphasis Training

Receiving and passing high balls
The players stay in groups of two.
- The ball is passed as a high ball and brought under control.
- Both partners juggle with the ball in the air between them.
- The ball is passed as a high ball over a long distance. The players take care that their movements are accurate and the balls are aimed correctly. The partner tries to bring the ball under control cleanly.
- A high ball is delivered as a pass from dribbling.

- With a high ball, Player A tries to tip Player B, who is trotting around some distance away.
- The idea now is to kick high balls over as long a distance as possible. The ball is always played back from the exact spot it was stopped at. Who can manage to force their partners back to the base line?

Putting it into Practice in a Game

A small four-a-side Soccer tournament takes place using two small goals and without anyóne in goal. Playing time is three minutes.
Round 1: Only low shots count as goals.
Round 2: Each goal headed earns double points.
Round 3: Each player can only score one goal.

Cool-Down run

ST 6

ST 7

Getting in the Mood/Warm-up

Warming up with a Tennis ball and a Soccer ball

By working with two different balls simultaneously one improves ball skills, concentration and coordination.
Each player has a tennis ball and a Soccer ball.
- The players dribble with the Soccer ball and and place the tennis ball on the palm of the hand, which is stretched out to the side.
- While dribbling with the Soccer ball, the tennis ball is thrown up and caught again.
- While the players are dribbling, the tennis ball is passed around the body.
- Stretching exercise: lying on their backs the players take hold of their shins and pull their legs towards their body. The head is raised up towards the knees.
- Stretching exercise: in an arched back position on the ground, one arm is stretched upwards and brought back down to the ground sideways.
- The players bounce both balls simultaneously.
- The Soccer ball is kicked ahead. The player tries to hit it with the tennis ball.
- The tennis ball is kicked forward using an inside pass. Then the Soccer ball is kicked in order to overtake the rolling tennis ball.

Emphasis Training

Taking shots at goal in competition situations

All players have a ball.
- The players dribble towards the manned goal and take a shot at it.
- They dribble towards the goal and have to out-dribble a defender – who is only playing with 50% effort – before taking a shot at goal.
- The above exercise is repeated from various different positions (centre, half-right, half-left).

The players form pairs. Each pair has a ball.
- The partners stand to the right and the left of the trainer on the halfway line. The trainer kicks the ball towards the goal. Both partners

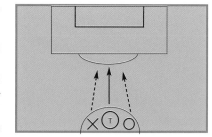

sprint after the ball and fight to get ball possession. The winner takes a shot at goal.

- Starting off the same way, this time running, the trainer keeps passing the ball to one player. The other player, however, has to try and get the ball from her before she takes a shot at goal.
- Both players stand behind each other on the halfway line. The player at the back throws the ball in the direction of the goal. Both sprint after it and fight to get ball possession; the winner takes a shot at goal.

Putting it into Practice in a Game

Game with a neutral player

This is a game with a majority/minority situation. The neutral player keeps on changing the team as she always plays in the team with ball possession.

Teams of seven are formed who now play 3:3 plus the neutral player.

- Goals can only be scored by way of a double pass.
- The goals scored by the neutral player are worth double points.
- A player may only pass the ball when she has dribbled her way past an opponent.

Cool-Down run

ST 8

Getting in the Mood/Warm-up

Stretching and strengthening with music

The warm-up phase takes place using music. A recorder with batteries as well as the appropriate motivating, rhythmical music is required. If announced a week or so beforehand, the players can bring their own music. Stretching and strengthening exercises can be done to music, but it is not always possible to do this to the right rhythm.

- The girls move to the rhythm of the music.
- They run to the rhythm of the music.
- They move their arms to the rhythm of the music.
- Legs and arms move in rhythm.
- Improvised movements to the rhythm of the music.

Strengthening exercises: lying on the stomach with arms stretched out in front; each arm is raised alternately.

- In a slightly straddled position, one places a hand up between the shoulder blades. The other hand pulls the elbow downwards from behind.
- In an arched back position on the ground, the outstretched right arm and left leg are raised up to a horizontal position and held for ten seconds. The same exercise is done with the other arm and leg.
- Lying on the back with legs bent, the lower legs are raised parallel to the floor. In this position the upper body is slightly raised and laid down again.
- The girls carry out 'wild' solo dancing moves to jazzy music.
- The music is stopped and the girls have to stay standing on one leg for about twenty seconds without moving.
- The next time the music is stopped the girls freeze into a funny monument and stay in this position for about ten seconds.

Emphasis Training

Header games

A heading game does not meet with a lot of enthusiasm amongst lower skilled players.

For this reason one should make a point of using light balls (softball, volleyball) to start off.

Each pair has a ball.
- The players head the ball to each other. The ball is first thrown up and then headed.
- Player A throws a high ball to B who heads it back immediately.
- The ball is passed in a drop kick shot. The partner tries to head the ball back.
- Two players try keeping the ball in the air for as long as possible by heading to each other. What pair manages six or even ten headers in one go?
- In a 1:1 heading game the players stand about 8 m apart opposite each other. Each game lasts 2-3 minutes. The winner moves on to the left, the loser stays where she is.

Putting it into Practice in a Game

Handball/Headers
Teams of four play a game using two goals and goalkeepers. Only headed goals count.
- Handball is played first. Just in front of the goal the ball is thrown to a player in such a way that she can score a goal with her head.
- Now Soccer. In front of the goal the ball must be kicked up a little in order for a player to manage to head the ball into the goal.

Cool-Down run

ST 9

Relays for warming up

Relays are becoming more and more popular because of their competitive character. Some little changes in the rules make it possible to adapt relays according to age and/or level of performance.

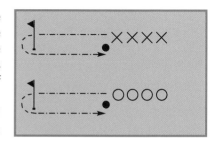

- A sprinting relay takes place around a turning mark. One can go for a dribbling or bouncing version.
- The course is now converted into a slalom circuit using flagpoles or traffic cones. Again the ball can be either bounced or dribbled here. Another alternative can be to kick the ball past the slalom circuit, then run through the circuit after it and finally bring it to a stop.

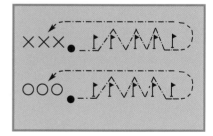

- In this relay, running speed is not the most important factor. Instead, certain tasks must be carried out at the individual flagpoles.
  Flag 1: The ball is bounced ten times with the right hand.
  Flag 2: The ball is juggled five times on the head.
  Flag 3: The ball is kept up in the air five times with the feet.
  Flag 4: The ball is thrown up five times and brought to a stop with the foot.

Hip-turn kick

The hip-turn kick is carried out as follows:
The player's upper body tilts out over the standing leg. The kicking leg swings round from the hip-joint horizontally against the ball.

Two groups of three are formed

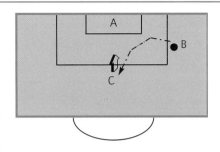

- Player A defends the goal. Player B throws the ball to C, who takes a shot at goal out of the air using a hip-turning manoeuvre. After several attempts the roles are reversed.
- Starting off as above, Player B plays a centre-pass in front of the goal and C converts this with a hip-turn kick. The quality of the centre-pass determines the other player's ability to take the hip-turn kick.

Putting it into Practice in a Game

Handball and Soccer

Teams of four or five are set up, including a goalkeeper.

- The teams play handball. In front of the goal the ball must be thrown in such a way as to allow the shooter to convert the ball using the hip-turn kick.
- Now they play Soccer. One point is earned when high balls in front of the goal are taken directly but no goal is scored. If a player manages to score a goal then it's worth three points.

Cool-Down run

ST 9

ST 10

Getting in the Mood/Warm-up

Hopscotch games

Hopscotch games improve coordination and strengthen jumping muscles. Girls enjoy them. Gymnastic hoops or coloured ribbons can be laid out as circles on the pitch.

- The players jump their way through the course doing standing and open jumps alternately.
- The course is completed in the same way this time followed by dribbling and a shot at goal to finish off.
- After completing the jumping course the players now have to run through a slalom circuit keeping the ball at their feet. The exercise finishes off with a shot at goal.
- The ball is kicked alongside the jumping course. The players then make their way through the course with standing jumps, later with the right and the left leg, On catching up with the ball they take a shot at goal.

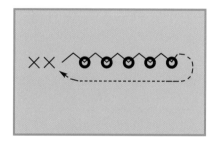

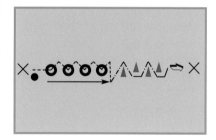

Emphasis Training

Improving techniques at station points

Various basic Soccer techniques are reinforced and improved using a station point system. They are set up around the sports field. At least two players can carry out their exercises at a station at the same time.

Station 1

The players dribble back and forth between two flagpoles. At each end they juggle the ball around.

Station 2

Player A throws or passes the ball to B who takes on the ball, dribbles with it for several metres and then kicks it back to A.

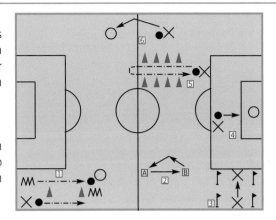

Station 3

Two goals are about 8 m opposite each other and two players head the ball to each other.

Station 4

The champion penalty-taker is what we're looking for here. Each player may take ten shots at the manned goal. Who scores the most goals?

Station 5

Both players make their way across the field doing throw-ins. The ball is always thrown from the spot where the player picked it up.

The exercises can go on for 2-3 minutes at each station. After each station the players have an active recovery phase and trot round the field before they go on to the next station.

Putting it into Practice in a Game

Zone game

The playing field is divided up into three areas. 5:5 is played in the middle area. In both of the goal zones there should be a ratio of three attackers: two defenders plus goalkeeper, so that a majority/ minority situation exists.

ST 10

- The players are allowed to use their hands in both goal zones, however, only for throwing the ball to a player to enable her to take a head shot at the goal.

- If an attacker can convert the ball to a goal using an inside kick, then the goal is worth double points.

Cool-Down run

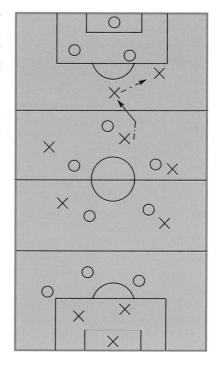

8.4 Offensive and Defensive Behaviour – Ten Training Sessions

Here in this chapter one can clearly see just how close training is to the real game. If one's team has ball possession they can go about the primary aim in Soccer i.e. scoring a goal. If the opposing team has the ball the aim now is to either prevent them from scoring a goal or win ball possession again as soon as possible.

> With these aims in mind there are certain practical skills and manoeuvres which have to be acquired. Some of them are listed below:
>
> * Improving overall game perception.
> * Developing a feeling for the layout on the field.
> * Improving the players' ability to play together.
> * Recognising and putting certain tactical features into practice.
> * Fulfilling particular task activities (e.g. marking a player).
> * Using certain game combinations (playing down the wing).
> * Being able to adapt quickly from an offensive to a defensive situation and vice versa.
> * Including the goalkeeper as the eleventh player on the field.

OD 1

Getting in the Mood/Warm-up

Individual work with the ball
Each player is working with a ball.
* The players dribble around freely.
* Dribbling takes place with the inside of the foot.
* The above exercises are done with the strong and weak foot.
* The ball is sent forward with an instep kick and caught up with again after a sprint.
* Stretching exercise: On all fours, the right arm is raised to the side and then brought in as far as possible under the left arm.
* On all fours, the left knee is brought to the forehead, held there, and then stretched out backwards. When stretching out the leg be sure to avoid having a hollow back!

- The players dribble the ball quickly. When the trainer gives a signal the players bring the ball to a stop with their feet, sit on it and then carry on dribbling.
- Keep the ball up in the air for as long as possible. One should also try using the heel in the process.

Emphasis Training

Tactics in majority and minority games
When certain tactical combinations are being taught, the trainer may interrupt a game immediately when they are not carried out properly. Only this way is it possible to rectify incorrect behaviour directly when it happens, e.g. running the wrong way.

- The players play 4:2 or 5:2, using two small goals and no goalkeeper. The team in the majority plays the game by only touching the ball twice. The minority team plays without any restriction because they are under pressure already from the opponents.
- In a 4:2 game, without a goalkeeper, the majority team may only score a goal when all four players have have played the ball beforehand. The minority team on the other hand are even allowed to use their hands. It's only when they're taking a shot at goal that they have to use their feet.
  Hint: The game can be stopped:
  − in order to confirm a good tactical move and strengthen it.
  − to point out incorrect behaviour and give the right solution.
  − to play a similar situation again, but this time with corrections.

Putting it into Practice in a Game

Game with two goals
A game takes place with two small goals and goalkeepers.

- Team A plays against B. A has to get the ball from their penalty area to the penalty area opposite without any opponent touching it.
  If they succeed the team wins a point. If they also manage to score a goal they get double points. Team B meanwhile should try and put the opposing team under pressure by covering and marking their opponents.

Cool-Down run

OD 2

Getting in the Mood/Warm-up

Working with the ball in pairs

Pairs are formed. Each pair has a ball.

- The players pass the ball to their partners, first by bringing the ball to a stop, dribbling and kicking it, and then with direct passes.
- While passing the ball to each other on the move, the distance between the players is increased and reduced. The ball is passed directly.
- During the passing movements the tempo is increased so that there is a good bit of drive on the ball.
- The players stand up straight, stretch their arms up over their head and press the palms of their hands together as tightly as possible.
- Lying on the back the outstretched right leg is raised up into a vertical position. At the same time the left hand is brought towards the right knee and pushes against using maximum strength. The right hand is lying flat on the ground.
- Player A passes the ball to B, sprints after it and tries to win the ball back again.
- Player A passes the ball to B who in turn must now get past Player A again.
- In a 1:1 game using two small goals without a goalkeeper, a goal can only be scored when a player has succeeded in getting past her opponent at least once.

Emphasis Training

Improving overall game perception

In a marked out playing area of 30 x 20 m, two teams of seven play with a ball. Each team has a ball.

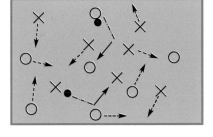

- Each player in a team has a number and all players are moving around the area. The ball must be passed to each other in numerical order (1,2,3 etc).
- The ball is passed in descending numerical order. Each player is only allowed to touch the ball twice.
- The ball may now be passed randomly; but all players must have played the ball after seven passes.

- Each team now plays with two balls at the same time, which means that total concentration and good overall perception is required. A player must never receive both balls at the same time.

Putting it into Practice in a Game

Tactical training
A game of 7:7 with two neutral players is played.
- On a marked out playing field of 50 x 30 m, the team in ball possession tries to dribble past one of the two base lines; the other team tries to prevent this and get ball possession themselves. The two neutral players always play with the team in ball possession.
- Now the teams play using two goals, each with a goalkeeper. This time the two neutral players support both teams in defence. They therefore not only have to keep changing teams but also have to run from one goal to another to help the other defenders. This is a very exerting task where frequent role reversals are necessary.

Cool-Down run

OD 3

Getting in the Mood/Warm-up

Warming up with a paper cup and a Tennis ball

Each player has a tennis ball and a paper cup. The cups are laid out around the marked out playing field.

- The players run forwards, backwards, in a side gallop and a hop-and-run around the cups.
- The players trot around and jump over the cups, imitating a heading movement.
- The players run around the cups bouncing the tennis ball.
- Lying on the stomach, the abdomen and posterior are tensed, the left arm and the right leg are pressed down against the ground. The players raise their right arm and left leg by about 1 cm and stay in this position for about ten seconds.
- Lying on the back, the players do cycle movements with their legs.
- The tennis ball in the cup is jetted up and caught again with the cup. Don't forget to change hands!
- The cups together with the tennis balls are laid out around the field. Who has managed to hit all of them with the ball and is now sitting in a corner of the field?
- The players run a there-and-back relay. In the first part the ball is carried in the cup. At the turning point the ball is jetted into a basket and has to stay in it before the player can run back.

Emphasis Training

The game: 6 + 1 against three

First of all a playing area of 20 x 15 m is marked out. Six players of Team A stand scattered around outside the playing area. Another member of Team A is in the playing area in ball possession and plays against the Team B three members. Team A's field player is allowed to pass the ball to a teammate outside, who must pass it back to her. This is exactly what the players of Team B try to hinder. If Team B manages to get ball possession, the three players pass the ball to each other as often as possible, whereas the player on her own tries to win it back. Each successful pass is worth one point for each team.

- The following rule can be used as an alternative: the players on the field are allowed as much contact with the ball as they like, the outside players however may only have contact with the ball twice.

After every two minutes the centre players should be changed as they are exerting themselves a lot.

Improvements in passing and covering
The girls play a game of 8:4 in an area of about 30 x 20 m.
- The majority team have to try and keep possession of the ball for as long as possible. However the ball must be kept low. A point is only awarded after ten passes in a row. The minority team earn a point when they manage to break down the opposing team's chain of passes before the tenth pass.
- The game is played under the same conditions, with one exception. The team in majority has to send high passes to each other this time.

Cool-Down run

OD 4

Getting in the Mood/Warm-up

Exercises with the medicine ball
The medicine balls are laid out around the field.
- The players run around the balls.
- Then they jump over the balls.
- The players run around the field as they like. If they come to a ball they pick it up, throw it up in the air, catch it, put it back down on the ground again and run on.
- While running around, the balls are this time picked up and are thrown away with a two-handed movement.
- Stretching exercise: The players sit cross-legged, the soles of the feet are touching each other. The knees are pushed down to the ground by the elbows.
- Stretching exercise: Lying on the stomach, the left hand pulls the left leg towards the bottom. The forehead is leaning on the back of the right hand. Change sides!
- While trotting around the players dribble with the medicine ball for a little and then leave it lying again.

Several relays with the medicine ball complete this warm-up:
- The ball is rolled around the floor using the hand.
- The ball is dribbled through a flagpole alley.
- The ball is moved along using two-armed throws.

Emphasis Training

Technical-tactical training at station points
Up to six players can train at any station at the same time. One can play for up to ten minutes at each station. After that comes stretching, loosening up and relaxed trotting before moving on to the next station.
- Station 1
  The girls play 3:3 with two small goals and no goalkeeper. Girl versus Girl is what's practised here.
- Station 2
  The players run towards the penalty area and receive balls from the left or the right on the move. Using a direct shot they now have to get the ball into the manned goal. This training concentrates specifically on coordination and on shots at goal.

- Station 3

  In a majority/minority game of 4:2 with two small goals, various tasks have to be completed. The team of four always have to use their feet; the team of two have to use their feet in defence but are able to use their hands and score goals this way in attack.

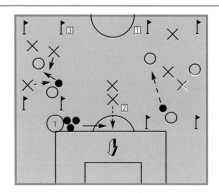

Putting it into Practice in a Game

Games emphasising various elements

Two teams play using two large goals and goalkeepers. The following points are emphasised:

- Double passes are to be played as often as possible. Every double pass earns one point, every goal earns five.
- The attackers should centre the ball as high up as possible in front of the goal. Every header attempted earns one point. A header, which ends up in the net, is worth three points.
- The forwards should attack as often as they can from the flank. Every centre in front of the goal is worth one point, every goal earns three points.

Cool-Down run

OD 4

OD 5

Training in groups of five
- The group of five pass the ball freely to each other. Each player, as soon as she has the ball, tries to fit in a few tricks.
- The group play direct double passes to each other.
- The five players keep the ball up in the air.
- The ball is passed over long distances by using drop kicks and instep kicks.
- Stretching exercise: with a straight back and a fixed pelvis, the lower leg is pulled up towards the bottom.
- Stretching exercise: starting off in a kneeling position with the hands on the hips, one leg, laying on the ground, is moved forward. The upper body is then straightened up.
- The group of five now passes two balls to each other at the same time.
- The group of five forms a large circle and pass both balls to each other, one after another. The ball must be passed on as quickly as possible.
- The group of five practise dummy moves. The girl with the ball calls out another player's name, doesn't pass the ball to her but rather to another girl instead. The circle can be made smaller for this to increase the element of surprise. The game can also be played using eye contact.

Emphasis Training

2 + 1:2 with small goals
This is a 2:2 game with normal goals and goalkeepers.
- The neutral player always reinforces the team attacking. The attackers must run free after each pass so that they are in a position for the ball to be passed back to them again. The defenders don't mark a player but rather the area in front of the goal.
- The neutral player plays on the same side as the attackers, but she has a 'setting-up' role and stays behind the forwards. She tries to give them low passes into the free zone. This time both defenders each mark an opposing player. The 'setting-up' player does not need to be marked as she may not score goals.
- Starting position is as above. However, this time the neutral player has to pass semi-high and high balls to the forwards.

Putting it into Practice in a Game

Games with emphasis on tactics
The players play on a full-sized pitch with two goals and goalkeepers.
- Goals only count under the following conditions: the ball must be passed by a defender down the flank and centred in front of the goal with a cross pass.
- A goal is only counted as a success when it is passed by a midfield player to an attacker, who finishes off with a shot at goal.
- The normal rules basically hold here. However, the defenders can also win a point when they manage to prevent the opponents from making centres.
- This time the defenders have to intercept low passes if they want to gain a point for their team.

Cool-Down run

OD 6

Getting in the Mood/Warm-up

Partner work with the medicine ball
The players form pairs, each pair has a ball.
- While trotting around a prescribed area the players throw the medicine ball to each other with a swing, to the left and to the right.
- On the move, the ball is hit across to the partner using one arm.
- The ball is hit across using both arms.
- A player throws the ball forwards, both players sprint after it and fight to get ball possession.
- Starting off on all fours; the right arm is stretched up out to the side. Then the right arm is guided in under the left arm.
- Standing slightly straddled, the arms are stretched upwards and the girls press the palms of their hands together as hard as possible.
- The players throw the ball to each other in 'throw-in' style.
- In a scramble for the ball each player tries to get ball possession and then place the ball on a particular spot.
- The players stand opposite each other. One girl has the ball jammed between her feet and jets the ball to her partner with her legs.

Emphasis Training

Games with majority/minority situations
Teams of three are formed, each playing against one of three little goals. Each player then has a goal to attack and a goal to defend.

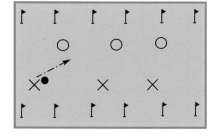

- A further player is in action in front of the three in defence. This means that she is constantly changing sides as she always plays for the team who is defending.
- The freelance player strengthens the offensive, irrespective which team is attacking. She plays behind the three forwards, however, bringing them into the best possible position. She herself is not allowed to score any goals. Her passes should stay low where possible and be kicked up into the open.

- The freelance player is changed after three minutes at the latest due to the exerting demands on her.

Putting it into Practice in a Game

Not much ball contact, direct passes
A game takes place using normal goals with goalkeepers. After each three minute session, the playing rules are changed.

- Rule 1
  A player is not allowed to have contact with the ball more than three times in a row.
- Rule 2
  The ball is kept down low. High balls mean the opponents get a free kick.
- Rule 3
  The ball is passed on with one touch of the ball, i.e. direct passes.
- Rule 4
  Passes must be under 5 metres.
- Rule 5
  The girls can play as they like, without any restrictions.

Cool-Down run

OD 7

Getting in the Mood/Warm-up

Playing stations with the Soccer ball

Each player has a ball. They run through several stations where they practise varous things .

- Station 1
  Numerous obstacles (balls, sports bags, jackets, T-shirts etc.) are laid out in a marked out area. Each girl practises juggling the ball in their own particular way.
- Station 2
  The girls send the ball out in front of them with a drop kick, sprint after it and dribble through a slalom course.
- Station 3
  The players have to send the ball with a low shot through a traffic cone lane which gets narrower as it goes on, then sprint after the ball and catch it up again.
- Station 4
  The players start off having to kick the ball under four hurdles, which are standing behind each other. They have to jump over the hurdles and catch up with the ball. On the way back they kick the ball under one hurdle, jump over this hurdle, kick the ball under the next hurdle, jump over that hurdle etc.

Emphasis Training

A neutral 'Gamemaker'

Teams of four are formed and they play with small goals and no goalkeeper. One neutral player helps the team in ball possession. She may not be attacked by the defending team, so that she can concentrate on playing accurately.

- The neutral player kicks the ball down the open field and the attacking forwards have to run to get it.
- The neutral player must play the ball to a forward in such a way that the ball is passed on the rebound back to her, who then tries to take a shot at goal.
- The neutral player passes high or medium-high balls up the field. The attacking forwards bring the ball under control and finish the whole thing off with a shot at goal.
- The neutral player has to play double passes with the attacking forwards repeatedly.

Putting it into Practice in a Game

Playing with teams of different sizes
The girls decide themselves how they want to play. The teams have between three and five members. The game takes place with small goals and no goalkeepers. Playing time is five minutes each round. When two different-sized teams meet each other, a certain score is set from the start e.g. in a 3:5 game, the game starts with a score of 2:0 for the smaller team. However in the game itself all goals are worth two points.

- Round 1
  Every goalscorer must run through the goal with the ball at her feet. Balls that are shot from far away don't count.
- Round 2
  A shot at goal must be taken from at least eight metres for it to count.
- Round 3
  The goals are widened to five metres and goalkeepers are used. A goal scored with the strong foot is worth one point, with the weak foot two and with a header three.

Cool-Down run

OD 8

Getting in the Mood/Warm-up

Relays using other apparatus

The players are divided up into three teams who now run relays against each other.

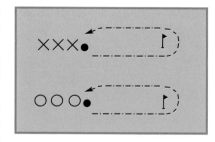

- The players dribble around a turning point. The ball must stay close to the foot at all times.
- This time the players dribble there and back with a different ball e.g. a rugby ball, a tennis ball or a medicine ball.
- This time the girls have to do three rounds of dribbling. On the second round a tennis ball is also balanced on the flat palm of the hand, on the third round the girls must dribble with a Soccer ball and a light medicine ball.
- Stretching exercise: on all fours, put the right knee on the ground, the left knee is moved forward towards the forehead. Then the left leg is stretched out behind. Avoid a hollow back!
- Starting off lying on the back, the right leg is stretched up in the air as vertical as possible. The left hand presses hard against the right knee. The right arm is lying alongside the body.
- The relay distance is reduced to about five metres. The players now balance the ball in one hand over this distance and back.
- This relay can also be done using headers.

Emphasis Training

Playing down the flank, counter-attack, shifting play

One half of the pitch is used for playing. A player is in goal. Two little goals are set up on the halfway line on the side-lines.

- Team A plays towards the goalkeeper in the main goal, and at the same time defends the two little goals. Team B does exactly the opposite.
  The main emphasis for Team A is to practise playing down the wing and the organisation of the defence in front of the two little goals. Team B concentrates mainly on quick attacks on the small goals, the necessary field layout for this as well as the organisation of the defence in front of the main goal.

- Starting off with the same conditions as above there is now a change in play. Team A now use short passes in attack in front of the main goal. Team B shift their attacks from the right goal to the left or the other way around. The players have to recognise where the better goal chances are.

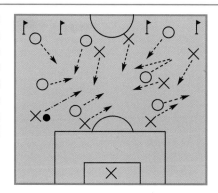

Putting it into Practice in a Game

Playing with four small goals
The game takes place with each team playing against two small goals without goalkeepers. The goalkeepers play as normal players so that they can work on and improve their playing style.
Four little goals are set up in a playing area. Team A takes over the offensive role and may attempt ten attacks. Team B is defending. Then the roles are changed over. Which team was able to finish off the most attacks with a goal?

Cool-Down run

OD 9

Getting in the Mood/Warm-up

Catching games with and without a ball
- A simple catching game is played in the penalty area.
- While playing catch in the penalty area, a softball is passed between players. The player in possession of the ball cannot be tagged.
- The players pass a Soccer ball backwards and forwards. The game of catch takes place at the same time. The girl in ball possession is safe, however, she must pass the ball on immediately.
- Stretching exercise: With a straight back and a fixed pelvis, the players pull their lower leg up to their bottom.
- Lying on their backs, the girls grasp their shins and pull their thighs in to the body. The head moves forward towards the knees.
- The players move around in the penalty area. Two catchers pass the ball to each other and try to hit the others (soft ball).
- Two players stand about 8 m opposite each other in the middle of the field. The other players change ends, and run through this bottleneck. The pair with the ball try to hit a runner.

Emphasis Training

Bringing players into position
A game takes place on one half of the pitch using two goals with goalkeepers. The playing area is divided up into three zones. In both areas in front of the goals, the players play 3:3. In the midfield zone this ratio is 3:1.

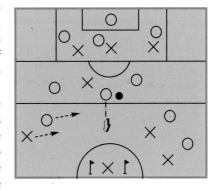

While the teams play as normal in the two goal zones, there are different rules for the midfield zone. The team of three only play offensively when they try to bring their attackers into more favourable positions using accurate passes. The player on her own has to try and prevent such a good pass. When the smaller team i.e. the team with one midfield player, has ball possession, the players in the middle zone are not allowed to be attacked. She can bring her attacking team colleagues into the game easily, using a skilful pass.

Putting it into Practice in a Game

Passing combinations
Two teams are formed.
- In a marked out area of the field, Team A passes the ball with the hand to each other as often as possible and without the opposing team interrupting them. Ten passes are worth one point. Team B has to prevent this and manage as many passes as they can themselves.
  The ball is allowed to touch the ground.
- In the second round the rules are tightened. The ball may not touch the ground now. If it does, the other team gets ball possession.
- Both teams – each member of Team A has a ball – stand on the halfway line area about ten metres opposite each other. After a signal, the girls in possession, dribble toward the opposing team and try to reach the goal line opposite with their ball. How many players manage this?

Cool-Down run

OD 9

OD 10

Getting in the Mood/Warm-up

Hunting ball in various forms
The penalty area is used for this game.
- One player in the team is nominated to be the hunter, all other players are rabbits. The hunter tries to tag the rabbits who are running around freely.
- This time there are two hunters. They have a ball between them (soft ball) which they aim at the rabbits. The hunters can pass the ball to and fro to each other until a good opportunity arises.
- The two hunters now have a ball each. Each hunter uses his feet. The rabbits now have to jump up a lot if they want to avoid getting hit as all balls have to be kicked down low.
- Stretching exercise: the players sit cross-legged. The soles of the feet are touching each other. The knees are pressed down to the ground with the elbows.
- Stretching exercise: one hand grasps the other wrist behind the back and pulls it down sideways.
- Two hunters are bounding around again. One hunter kicks low passes and the other has to try and hit the players using a bounced ball.

Emphasis Training

Game with 'Out-of-Bounds' zones
Two teams are formed. A line is drawn parallel to the side-lines about five metres away from them on both sides. In the middle zone the teams play 5.5 up to 7:7. However, one attacker is playing in each of the two outer zones. She has the task of giving both teams well-timed centre passes in front of the goal. As she has no direct opposing players, she has enough time to send accurate centre passes in front of the goal. 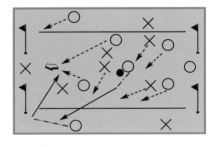 Therefore what's being practised here is playing down the wing, taking flanking passes and headers. In defensive situations one concentrates on the distribution of players on the field, marking a player as well as the interception of centre passes.

Putting it into Practice in a Game

Defence and attack in the goal area

The girls play against one goal, with a goalkeeper. One can form teams of 6:6 up to 9:9.

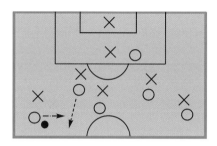

- The members of each team receive a number. Players with the same number have the task of neutralising each other. When a team is attacking, the forwards have to keep on freeing themselves from their markers and vice versa.
- Particularly important now are through shots from behind. The ball is passed to the forward attackers, but they play the ball back to another player who then takes a moving shot at goal.

Cool-Down run

8.5 Standard Situations –
Three Training Sessions

Standard situations are becoming more and more important in modern Soccer. When a team cannot manage to score a goal in the course of the game they then rely on standard situations and the special talents of individual players. There is, however, one thing common with all three standard situations: the game has stagnated, and from this situation the ball is passed into or in front of the goal. This gives the attacking team the opportunity to take well thought out action under no pressure, whereas the defending team can only react.

The ability to take advantage of such a situation is a significant characteristic of today's Soccer. Teaching these standard situations is easy, but there are certain essential requirements for them to work successfully in practice.

- Standard situations, which are carried out quickly, come as a surprise for the opposing team.
- The game play must be determined beforehand.
- Similarly, ball direction and passing moves must also be laid down beforehand.
- Timing between the respective players must be perfect.
- Particularly talented players take over certain duties and carry them out accurately.

The opposing team will certainly try to work out the attackers' intentions as early as possible in order to be in a position to react appropriately. As well as this they will try to eliminate the specialists.

Every player, however, is expected to mentally tackle these standard situations — both in the offensive and defensive. The practical way of learning them goes from trying things out through to rehearing situations up until they come automatically. This could be one way of learning them:

- The trainer and the players lay down possible variations which can be carried out according to the inherent player potential (e.g. a good header) and technical abilities.
- The technical sequence (without and then with opponent) is practised first in the training session, perhaps either in one-to-one or group training.
- Once the players master the technicalities, the whole sequence of events is worked on with all players.
- It's only at this stage that the situation in question is included in the emphasis training phase. 'Corner' training with the whole team only makes sense when 'nearly all' balls do actually end up landing in front of the goal.

The structure for the standard situations differs from the previous ones.

- Throw-in
- Corner
- Free Kick

For each themeonly one training session is described quite comprehensively and can be frequently included in emphasis training.

SS 1 The Throw-in

The throw-in has had a miserable history in Soccer for decades. In today's game, however, the throw-in first of all means that one's own team has ball possession. Not only this, but a throw-in, which takes place near the corner flag can offer real goal chances. The proviso, however, is that specialists have emerged in the team, who are able to carry out long accurate throw-ins as well as dangerous centre passes in front of the opponent's goal.

Getting in the Mood/Warm-up

Hand work with the ball
Each player has a ball; the ball itself can vary in form (Soccer, handball, medicine ball, volleyball etc.). After doing an exercise three times a player swops with another player.
- The players throw the ball in with a swing, reaching it across the whole field.
- They throw the ball across the field like a shot-put in athletics.
- The players throw the ball, this time as a throw-in, again reaching across the field.
- The players stand in a large circle. In the middle of this circle is a hoop. The players, using a throw-in style, must now aim to get the ball into this circle.
- The players must throw the ball in as far as possible. Each player has at least ten attempts.
- Working in partners, a player throws the ball in such a way that her partner can bring the ball to a stop easily with her foot.

Emphasis Training

The playing field can be made smaller when doing the following exercises with 'beginners' in order to ensure that the throw-ins are done accurately.
- The ball is thrown to a player on the field in such a way that she can take it on with her foot.
- The ball is thrown in such a way that the player on the field has to take it on with her body.
- The ball is thrown in such a way that the player on the field has to take it on with her head.
- These exercises are practised on the spot, on the move and with moderate defence from another player.

Different variations of a throw-in directly in front of the goal are as follows:

- **Variation 1**
  The ball is thrown in to the midfield player who is standing near the goalpost. She in turn heads the ball on further so that the players waiting behind can manage to score a goal with a header.

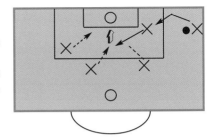

- **Variation 2**
  Player 1 throws in to Player 2. She heads the ball to 3 who then takes a volley shot at goal.

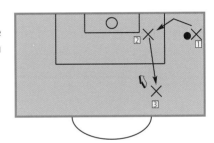

- **Variation 3**
  Players 2 and 3 start running towards the player doing the throw-in (1) in order to confuse the opposing players. But then Player 1 throws the ball in skilfully over 2 and 3 to oncoming Players 4 and 5.

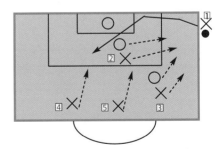

- **Variation 4**
  Player 1 throws in to Player 2, who heads the ball back to 1. Now 1 sends a centre pass in front of the goal to the Players 3 and 4.

  The basic patterns practised here can be varied and supplemented according to individual requirements.

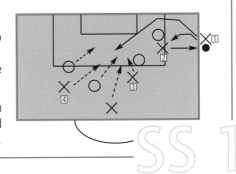

Putting it into Practice in a Game

The team divides up into pairs and each pair has a ball.
- The pairs throw the ball in to each other and move around the playing field in this way. The ball is thrown back from the spot it was caught each time.
- Both players now stand in the opposing goals. One selects a distance where it is possible to score a goal with a throw-in. In this way each player practises throwing-in as well as being goalkeeper.
- A third player comes along who situates herself near the goal on either side and receives the ball through a throw-in. She then tries to score a goal with a header or a kick.
- Finally a free game takes place with the whole team on the full pitch. A goal scored following a throw-in is worth three points.

Cool-Down run

SS 2 The Corner

Many games have been decided in the last minute thanks to a successfully converted corner. 'Corners' are then particularly successful when the team has a specialist for sending the ball in and several good players who can do headers in front of the goal. A player can also be successful by simply reacting quickly and getting the ball over the line with her foot in an unclear situation.

One differentiates between the following basic forms of a corner:
- Corners where the ball angles away from the goal, i.e. the corner is played from the right with the right foot.
- Corners where the ball angles towards the goal, i.e. the corner is taken from the right with the left foot.
- Short corners aimed at the near post.
- Long corners aimed at the far post.
- Corners which are played short to a team mate, who then passes the ball back.

In order to carry out effective corner training, it is necessary to lay down target areas, the appropriate attackers (header specialists) and their routes. The essential requirement for precision in front of the goal is an accurate centre pass.

Getting in the Mood/Warm-up

High balls with a partner
The players divide up into pairs and each pair has a ball.
- The players send high balls to each other over a long distance. The ball is then brought to a clean stop before being passed back again.
- The ball is now passed directly.
- A partner demands a pass by sprinting to get a high ball on the move.
- Stretching exercise: starting off lying on the stomach, the upper body is raised with outstretched arms and lowered again.
- Stretching exercise: lying on the back, one leg is bent over the other while the head turns in the other direction. The arms are stretched out to the side.
- Both players send high balls to each other. These are stopped with the foot, the body or the head alternately.
- The balls are sent up so high that the partner has to jump up to reach them with her head.

Emphasis Training

Basic pattern for a corner

- Variation 1

  This is a corner which ends up turning away from the goal. The movements and target zones for those players who are to convert the corner must be laid out beforehand. The centre passes must come in as accurately as possible in front of the goal so that the attackers have ample opportunities for making a goal shot or a header.

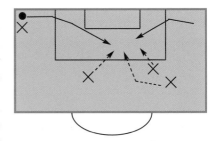

- Variation 2

  The corner is played towards the near post and then passed on by Player 1. Players 2 and 3 now have the chance of scoring a goal.

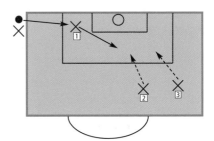

- Variation 3

  Players 1, 2 and 3 run towards the near post in order to mislead the defenders. The corner is aimed at the far post, however, and can be converted by Players 4 and 5.

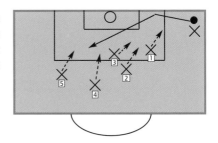

- Variation 4

  The ball is played at the near post with a low hard shot. The attackers try to convert the ball directly.

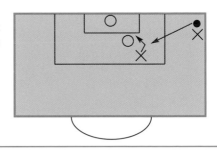

Putting it into Practice in a Game

Corner – Goal
- Teams of six take part in a 'corner competition'. All teams are against each other. Within each team the tasks are constantly swopped. A goalkeeper is standing in goal. A player kicks ten corners at goal. The other five players convert them into goals.
  Alternative: One player sends the corners in front of the goal, three players convert them into goals, two players try to prevent this.
- In the 'Corner – Goal' game both goals with goalkeeper are relatively close to each other (e.g. the second goal is on the edge of the penalty area). Each team takes six corners alternately. After each corner shot the teams continue playing until one of the teams scores a goal. In this way the players have to concentrate on defence and offence in corner situations alternately.
- In a free game, each ball that goes out over the line leads to a corner for the team instead of a throw- in.

Cool-Down run

SS 3 The Free Kick

One remembers well all the big names of those who have shot their team to victory with a free kick in a vital match. These free kick specialists shine mainly by virtue of their perfectly angled or hard shots and the proof of their skills lies in the strike. Free kicks, however, can also be used to lay the ball on for the other players in numerous ways.

The rule book makes a difference between direct and indirect free kicks. The direct free kick may be taken at goal without any further ball contact, this is not the case with the indirect one. As well as this we have the special form of the direct free kick – the penalty kick. Free kicks outside the penalty area are dealt with in the following section.

There are two possible variations of a free kick:
- The player tries to score a goal with a direct shot. The remaining players don't seem to be involved at all. However this is not true. They are there to confuse their opponents with their running around and keep the line of fire free. The player taking the free kick can then plan to take a hard shot directly on target or to put spin on it.
- In the case of an indirect free kick the other players are actively involved in the whole thing, but with different functions. The ball is either passed on target to them in open areas or in the direction they're running, or alternatively they lead the defenders away from the central line of attack by running around, thus making room for the player with the ball.

- Variation 1
The ball is kicked around the wall using the left or right foot, heading for the goal corner in question at low or medium height level.

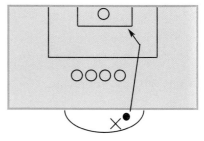

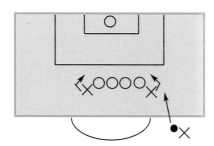

- Variation 2
Players are standing to the right and left of the wall. The player taking the free kick passes the ball to them, they do a half-turn and take a shot at goal.

Alternative: In addition to this, two attackers confuse their opposing players by running around – crossing in front of the wall.

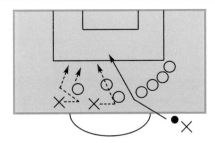

- Variation 3:
  The ball is kicked up over the wall and taken on by a player standing next to the wall who then takes a shot at goal.

- Variation 4:
  As the player runs up to take her free kick, the players standing in front of the wall run away to the side in order to draw their opposing players along with them and thus create a gap in the wall for the free kick.

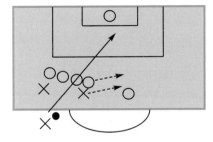

Putting it into Practice in a Game

In a free kick competition the goals are set up 35-40 m opposite each other.
- Every thirty seconds the trainer interrupts the game and the team who have ball possession are awarded a free kick from where the ball happens to be at that moment. As the goals are close to each other this means that every free kick is dangerous. In this way simultaneous offensive and defensive behaviour is worked on.
- In a free game, all interruptions such as a foul, ball out etc are punished with a free kick. Each free kick is repeated three times, however, a different player takes the free kick each time.

Cool-Down run

9 SCORING GOALS – PREVENTING GOALS

If one were to give a simple explanation of the idea behind the game of Soccer, it would be short and sweet: To score goals and prevent goals! And these two aims must be taken into consideration in every training sesssion. In order to give the trainers more of a feeling for this task, we have put together the following exercises and games which can be supplemented or varied where necessary. This is purely a collection of exercises which are quite complex in nature in some cases.

Exercise 1

- The goalkeeper runs through a slalom course, sprints into the goal and saves a ball which has been shot by another player.
- The goalkeeper runs through a slalom circuit, this time running around each slalom pole, sprints into the goal and saves the balls shot by three players in a row. These shots can vary in form.
- The goalkeeper runs through a slalom course, does a forward roll at each slalom pole, sprints into the goal and saves the low balls shot by three players in a row.

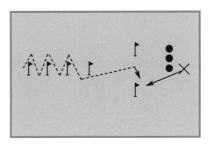

Exercise 2

- The goalkeeper runs through a slalom course, sprints into the goal and saves three high balls which are shot at the goal in a row, then sprints zigzagging along a path of hoops into a second goal, to save three successive low balls.

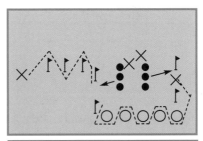

Exercise 3

- The goalkeeper is guarding two goals which are standing opposite each other. In the first goal three high balls are thrown in which she

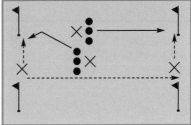

144

has to save. Then she sprints towards the other goal and this time clears three low shots.
- **Alternative:** Instead of throwing balls the players can also kick in centres or corners in front of the goal.

Exercise 4
- The goalkeeper intercepts a centre coming from the left, then clears a frontal shot, and finally intercepts a centre from the right.

Exercise 5
- The players take long shots at the goal from various positions. The sequence of shots should be quick enough to keep the goalkeeper in motion the whole time.

Exercise 6
- The players send in continuous centres from both sides in front of the goal – high and low – which are to be converted into goals by other players. The goalkeeper clears the balls.
- **Alternative:** The goalkeeper is supported by a defender.

Exercise 7
- The goalkeeper clears five successive shots at goal taken from Position 2, then sprints to Point A and clears five shots accurately to Position 3 before sprinting back into the goal to fend off five shots coming from Position 3.
- **Alternative:** This exercise could be repeated the other way round.

Exercise 8
- Groups of three are formed. Player A dribbles the ball and plays a double pass with B. After that A passes the ball to C, who in turn rebounds it back to A again. A then takes a shot at goal.

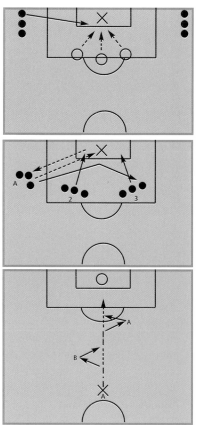

- **Alternative:** A dribbles round with the ball and plays a double pass with B. Player C is now in defence so that a 1:1 situation arises. A tries to get around C and take a shot at goal.

Exercise 9

- Player A dribbles at speed and passes the ball to B. Player B in turn picks up the ball, throws it up to A who in turn heads it to C. C passes the ball back to A again and A now takes a shot at goal.

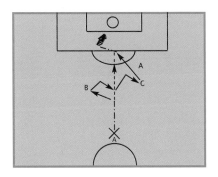

Exercise 10

- Player A kicks the ball carefully past a line of poles, and jumps over each pole. Then she takes on the ball and takes a shot at goal B. The goalkeeper picks up the ball, throws it in the direction that A is running. A now dribbles her way through a slalom course finishing off with a shot at goal C.

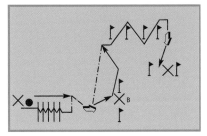

Exercise 11

- In the middle of a field four goals are set up to form a square. One goalkeeper guards all four goals. Outside this area up to six starting positions are laid out where players are standing with a ball each. The trainer calls out a number. The first player at this particular starting position dribbles towards the goal and tries to score a goal. When the trainer calls out the numbers quickly in turn the goalkeeper has to react quickly and run from one goal to another in order to be ready for the incoming shots.

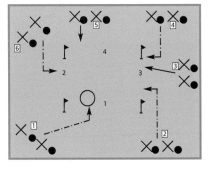

- **Alternative:** The attackers change over to the next group after taking their shot.

10 EASING OFF – COOL-DOWN

Soccer players should make a habit of doing a cool-down; something which doesn't happen enough in practice. It should be done after every training session not to mention after every match. Training normally finishes with a play element, which the girls enjoy and, in which they take part intensively. It's particularly relevant after a competitive game, where the players have exerted themselves for ninety minutes up until the final whistle.

This is what a Cool-Down does
- Body temperature is reduced slowly to its initial level, so that cardiovascular and muscular functions don't fall too suddenly.
- The muscles relax due to the reduction in the muscle tonicity caused by tiredness.
- The emittance of acidic, metabolic intermediate products is activated.
- The regeneration period after sporting exertion is shortened so that the entire regenerative process improves both quantitatively and qualitatively. The more often the teams have training and play matches the more significant this aspect becomes.
- By moving all the joints round, even if only just a little, the strain is taken off the spinal column and the cartilage around the joints. This enables fluid intake for the connective tissue. This process minimizes later damage to the spine and joints.
- A cool-down improves the players' general well-being; a feeling that they can really experience. At the same time it serves as a positive stimulus for the next session.

This is what to do in a cool-down
1 Easy, relaxed running and trotting
2 Shaking out and loosening of the limbs
3 Here and there a few low-intensity exercises for the whole body
4 A few light stretching exercises
5 Simple passing of the ball
6 Easy movement games with no competitive nature

This active cool-down can be supplemented with passive measures such as massages and recovery baths.

11 THE NECESSARY ORGANISATION OF A SOCCER TOURNAMENT

Soccer tournaments have to be organised and should be as interesting and as much of an experience as possible for the participants. This is also true for girls' tournaments. Since the people responsible for such matters in girls' Soccer are still breaking new ground, they should take a look at the following tips and advice for planning such a tournament.

Depending on the age and number of players a pitch can be divided up in different ways for a tournament.

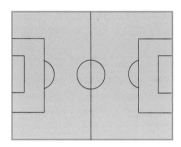

Normal pitch

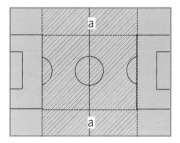

Small field from penalty area to penalty area (alternatively plus zones A)

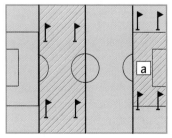

Two small playing fields lengthways (A alternative)

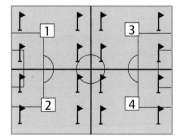

Four small fields, each field is a quarter of the whole pitch

In many cases such tournaments are on a fixed date in the year and take place every year. They are often given a specific name (Whit Tournament, St. Patrick's

Tournament etc) or are named after a famous person from the local or international area. As time goes on such tournaments can become a real tradition.

If you want to be really smart you can include specific rules in such a tournament. If the tournament takes place indoors for example, the ball has to be kept down low. When playing on a small pitch, one then uses goals that are only 2 m wide and no goalkeeper. These and other conditions give the tournament an interesting touch.

First comes the Planning

Before other teams are invited to the tournament one must consider several points beforehand.

- How many teams are to take part in the tournament?
- Over how many days should the tournament take place?
- Where (school, youth club, private) will the guest teams stay and be looked after?
- What is a good date? A weekend, a bank holiday or in the Soccer off-season?
- Where can the tournament take place? Are parallel games possible here?
- What form of play organisation should it be?
    - Four teams – playing each other
    - Six teams – two groups of three and finals
    - Eight teams – two groups of four with finals
- What age group is laid down on the invitation; how many players and substitutes are invited and are allowed to play?
- What are the incurring costs of such a tournament. How high should participant fees (per person) or starting money (per team) be?
- Can the organisers get some sponsors who would support the tournament with their donations (prizes, presents for the guests, food and drink) or money?
- How do the organisers find out the addresses of the teams to be invited?

When these questions are answered and the various club or school committees have given their approval, one can move on to the second step.

Now Is the Time for Preparation

The preparation phase starts off with the foundation of an organisation committee with all the people responsible for specific tasks. The committee immediately designates the people to take over the various duties.

- Applying for the use of the pitches during the event.

- Drawing up an announcement of the event explaining venue, date, age and number of the girls allowed to take part, type of tournament, playing time, game rules, accommodation, food and drink, costs, prizes, enrolment formalities and enrolment forms.
- Getting any necessary approval from authorities (Federation).
- Applying for the referees required.
- Sending off the invitations and the announcement to those teams meant to participate, setting a final date for receiving answers.
- Reserving accommodation and catering facilities.
- Sending confirmation of participation with timetable and plan to all guest clubs upon receiving their answer.
- Organising entertainment for all participating players, trainers, assistants, referees and organisers (tour of the town, sightseeing, dance or game evenings etc.).
- Appointing an escort for each guest team and referee.
- Appointing responsible people to take over the correspondence side, for the sports organisation, for the accommodation, catering and transport facilities required, for regulating the financial side of things and for the organisation of the entertainment programme.

Bringing the Event into the Limelight
- A patron is found for the event.
- An honorary board is set up with well-known/famous members. These support the tournament.
- Sponsors are found from the economy, trade, industry and business world, who help to support the tournament by donating gifts or money. (Receipts to be issued for these donations).
- The organisers inform the public media (daily newspapers, local papers, local radio and T.V) before, during and after the event.
- To make things easier for all people involved, the organisers keep a record of all necessary information and tasks.

Time	Activity	Responsible Person
12.01.03	Invitation of referees	Sharon Jones
14.02.03	Invitation of guests of honour	Jane Smith

Now it's Getting Serious

When all the preparation has been properly made, the tournament has been put on an optimum footing. Nevertheless the organisers need to possess certain skills and versatility in order to be able to counter any questions or hurdles which may suddenly arise.

- Each guest team is welcomed on their arrival and given a drink or small gift as a surprise. They are then brought to their quarters or to the sports field.
- All trainers and team assistants get together once more before the tournament begins and go through all procedures briefly.
- A control body may be set up with three to five responsible people, who watch the course of events during the tournament and pass a decision on any points of dispute where necessary.
- The tournament begins after a short opening ceremony with music, an official welcome and a sports demonstration.
- The teams shake each other's hands before each match. They then exchange club pennants.
- During the tournament it's a good idea to have the teams together and doing things together as much as possible so that the whole event has a positive atmosphere.
- Players who do not behave in a sporting manner are called to the players' board (five responsible players from various teams) to explain their behaviour.
- The tournament finishes off with a presentation ceremony where the donated cups and prizes are all awarded before the teams head off home.

A Brief Look Back at Things

There are two aspects in recapping on an event; the positive and the critical ones. Both are mentioned and are discussed and evaluated with regard to the total impression made.

- Each person involved briefly reviews the area they were responsible for.
- Suggestions are made for improving the critical points (structural, particular areas) and laid down in writing.
- Finally the book of records is revised, adapted or supplemented.

12 SPENDING LEISURE TIME TOGETHER AS A TEAM

Apart from training and matches together, every team needs additional activities for improving their feeling of togetherness. Being able to get on with each other is very beneficial to their activities in sport. The trainer and her assistants can offer to undertake something in their leisure time. As well as just 'Soccer' the girls also look for other opportunities to experience things together; as long as they feel comfortable within their team they will be reluctant to go without these close ties. Developing a "We belong together" feeling creates a sense of affiliation within the team and on the other hand also leads to improved harmony when it comes to sport.

Spending leisure time together is a qualitative requirement which is just as important for players in a team as training and playing levels. All elements together go to create each individual player's identity with her team. What brings the girls together? For young soccer players there are many reasons to want to do things together. In this, soccer related activities should be the centre of interest.

The Girls Celebrate Sporting Occasions
- Our young team has won their first match.
- A new player has come into the team. She celebrates her new start.
- The team won their first Soccer tournament.
- It's the trainer's birthday. The team organises a fun party after training
- The team has managed to move up a division in this season.
- The team scraped through this season and managed to avoid relegation.
- For the first time ever we beat our formidable opponent or local rivals. That just has to be celebrated!
- After a match against a particularly friendly opponent, an outing is arranged.
- The Soccer season is finished.

Private occasions can also be a good reason to have a get-together with the whole team provided of course that one wants to do this.

The Girls Celebrate Personal Occasions
- A player invites the team to her birthday.
- A girl in the team comes of age.
- A player has passed an important examination.
- A player invites the team to a garden, pool or basement party.
- The new grill is 'christened' by the team.

As the year goes by there are more and more occasions for getting together. Either all or a part of the team are involved in the preparations.

The Girls Celebrate Seasonal Festivals
* Included here are fancy-dress parties at Hallowe'en, dancing round the Maypole, a summer party in the garden or on the sports grounds, a pre-Christmas party in the clubhouse among others.
* The team is invited to dinner by a sponsor or parent.
* The team takes part in a dancing course together in the spring.
* The whole team visits a fairground or Christmas market together.

Many other situations arise which enable the team to undertake something together. The following suggestions can be supplemented with one's own ideas where possible or adapted as appropriate.

The Girls Have Ideas
* If a player's (or trainer's) birthday is coming up, the team think out an original ritual for congratulating her. For example they write a poem and sing it to a well-known melody. They present her with a funny present and the birthday child must carry out some humorous tasks. It all finishes off with a surprise guest or another surprise.
* The team visits a Soccer match in the regional or national division. Going to have a look at a different sport can also be interesting, e.g. gymnastics, badminton, volleyball or dancing.
* Two or three players organise a mystery tour together with the trainer. Nobody else knows the destination nor the programme. Before heading off the players receive the bare amount of information necessary.
* The players meet up in their leisure time for an aerobics, gymnastics or judo course.
* The team meets up for a grill party, cheese party or fondue evening, perhaps even in the forest, on their own sports grounds or in a player's garden. They all bring something practical with them and thus contribute to the success of the evening. It might be wise to decide beforehand who brings what etc.
* Pedestrian or cycling rallies are organised for the younger players through the woods. The girls divide up into pairs and solve the tasks set. At the finish there is a playground where everybody meets up.
* Girls really enjoy fashion shows. Maybe they can also visit a beauty farm and get tips for facial and body care after training and a match.

Sometimes the team would like to go on a trip. One-day trips or journeys for a few days reinforce the sense of affiliation in the team, not to mention the interesting destinations that can be seen.

Outings Together
- Boat journey across a lake, a river or a dam.
- Visit to an adventure playground.
- Raft or canoe trips for the brave ones.
- A pleasant evening around a log fire.
- Visit to an animal park, safari park or zoo.
- Visit to an open-air museum.
- A jaunt with a cart.
- A pony/horse-ride through forest and field.
- Helping out on a farm by looking after the animals or helping out with the harvest.
- Visit to an airport with a guided tour.
- Visit to a radio station, T.V. studio or film gallery.

PHOTO & ILLUSTRATION CREDITS

Cover Design: Birgit Engelen
Cover Photos: Sportpressefoto Bongarts, Hamburg
Photos: Klaus Bischops; Michael von Fisenne Fotoagentur, Aachen
Illustrations: Heinz-Willi Gerards, Tanja Dohr

LEGEND

T	Trainer
× ○	Players
●	Ball
⌐	Flag, Goal posts
–·–·–▸	Dribbling
——▸	Shot or Pass
∧∧∧	Juggling
– – – –▸	Running without the Ball
◉	Hoops
▲	Boundary Cones
∧ ∧ ∧ ∨ ∨ ∨	Alternating jumps
⋀▸ ●	Throw the ball up

Ready for the Match

Klaus Bischops/Heinz-Willi Gerards

**Soccer – Warming-up
and Warming-down**

In this book the authors provide
some 35 programmes for proper
warming-up and warming-down
for soccer. The programmes are
full of variety to avoid monotony
and are based around the game
of soccer itself, within a team
situation. The book proceeds
from a basic understanding of
the needs of every individual to
stretch and ease their muscles
and tendons, through a series of
simple games and exercises
using the football and other aids.

136 pages, 22 photos, 172 figures
Paperback, 5 3/4" x 8 1/4"
ISBN 1-84126-014-2
£ 8.95 UK/$ 14.95 US
$ 20.95 CDN/€ 14.90